SPARKS FROM ZION

DAVID RUBIN

Shiloh
ISRAELPress

Sparks From Zion
ISBN 978-0-9829067-6-7

Published by Shiloh Israel Press

www.ShilohIsraelChildren.org
www.DavidRubinIsrael.com
www.Facebook.com/DavidRubin.Shiloh.Israel

Contact The Author
David@ShilohIsraelChildren.org
1-845-738-1522

Contact The Publisher
sipress@ShilohIsraelChildren.org

For Orders
1-800-431-1579 (toll-free)

Book Development and Production
Chaim Mazo – chaim@docmazo.com

Cover Design and Layout
Christopher Tobias

Printed in Israel

To the brave young soldiers of Israel who have fought valiantly in the spirit of Joshua, despite the unfortunate defensiveness and the misguided hesitation of their political leadership.

Contents

Introduction

"What is it like to live under all that pressure?"

"Why don't you move to someplace safer?"

"How do you make sense out of the Israeli political system?"

"When will you guys be rebuilding the Temple?"

These are but a few of the many questions that I am frequently asked by my friends around the world about living in Israel. I also get some less friendly comments, mostly on my Facebook page, from the enemies of Israel and the Jewish people:

"You Jews are robbing Palestine from the Palestinians!"

"What kind of country attacks United Nations-run schools?"

This book is my response, not just to my concerned friends, but also to those who are hostile. Yes, it's true that you can't fully understand the challenges we face here in the Middle East without being here, living through all of the complexities of life in the world's most maligned country, and therefore, I have written this book to inform people who are not here, but want to understand the real facts on the ground.

Despite its rich history in Jerusalem, Israel is the only nation on the globe with a capital city that is not recognized by even one nation. Not even the United States is willing to show Israel that minimal respect, so the American Embassy remains in the relatively new city of Tel Aviv, rather than being moved to the city where the kings of Israel reigned and the prophets of Israel preached God's word.

At the same time, and quite paradoxically, Israel is passionately loved by so many people on every continent. The admiration for, and excitement about this idealistic young nation seems to be growing more every day, even though its detractors are becoming more and more aggressive in denouncing and defaming Israel on the world stage.

Meanwhile, the so-called Arab Spring that had raised so many unrealistic hopes in the West, imploded into an Islamic nightmare of new terrorist organizations that clearly state the eventual goal of so many terrorist veterans – the Islamic Caliphate – a contiguous Muslim domination of the entire world. Islam means submission and all nations would have to submit to the oppressive Islamic sharia law that validates wife-beating, child abuse, and discrimination against "the other," in addition to encouraging "Jihad" or holy war against non-Muslims, which is the highest precept in Islam. The concept of "Love your neighbor as yourself" is known to be the loftiest in Judaism and was also taught by a Jew from Bethlehem whose teachings Christians try to follow, but in Islam violence and submission rule the day. Virtually every terrorist organization in the world is Islamic and it's not an accident. It arises from the core of Islam, which is radical. The beheadings of ISIS may shock many, but it's only a symptom, albeit a frightening one, of the quest to take over Western civilization and create that Islamic Caliphate. Israel may be the immediate target of the Islamic terrorist organizations, but the entire free world is the end goal.

As an unofficial spokesman for Israel, I have no qualms about calling it as I see it, living as I do in the biblical heartland of Israel in a region in which we are surrounded by Islamic enemies, and so I feel compelled to warn the free world about the dangers on the horizon. Nonetheless, I am extremely optimistic about the future and am continuously infused with excitement about this great experiment in leadership that we call the reestablished nation of Israel.

Does that sound like a contradiction to you? Terrorism, wars, and beheadings don't exactly sound like a barrel of laughs, which brings to mind an appearance on a radio talk show a couple of years ago. I was called by the producer a few short minutes before my scheduled air time. In a friendly voice, he asked me how things were going in Israel, to which I replied, "Things are great. Every day in Israel is a new blessing and it's a privilege to live here." It was then time to go on the air, so for the next fifteen minutes, I fielded questions about the Iranian race for the nuclear bomb, the Hamas-Fatah unity talks, and the latest terrorist attack.

When the interview was over, the producer got back on the phone and said, "Mr. Rubin, it was great having you on and we'd love to have you back on again, but I have to ask you a question. You told me that living in Israel is a privilege every day, but then on the air, you proceeded to talk about all of these terrible problems that you have to confront in your country. Isn't that a contradiction?"

Well yes, but also no.

On one hand, life in Israel seems like one great paradox. We have all of these challenges and very real dangers, but we often feel that we are in the safest place on Earth. Is it just a feeling, an emotional desert mirage? That may well be. On the other hand, it all makes sense.

We have an expression in Hebrew – *Hakol L'Tovah* – which means – Everything is for good. Now that doesn't mean that everything that happens is good. We know that bad things happen to good people. What it means is that everything happens for a good reason.

As one who believes strongly in the mission of Israel to be "A Light Unto The Nations", I am convinced that the awesome challenges that we face are all intended for good. I also believe that the Almighty is watching carefully to see how we confront each of those challenges.

This book is an ever-so-slightly modified collection of articles and blogs, originally published on the Israel National News (Arutz Sheva) website and subsequently published elsewhere, in which I speak about the enormous geo-political challenges that Israel faces on the global stage and within.

I have written most of these articles in 2014, a difficult period of time during which Israel has been confronted with a resurgence of war and terrorism. Meanwhile, the rest of the free world has struggled with turmoil in the Islamic countries and the meteoric rise of ISIS, and all of this while the free world has lacked the political leadership to stand up to that challenge.

Much of the world is in great confusion today. An unrestrained secularism has created a values vacuum in Western society that the forces of Islam are aggressively trying to fill. Simultaneously, Israel is struggling with its own critical role, with many Israelis still trying to be "a nation like all the other nations," but this can never be, for Israel is destined to have a role of leadership in the world. The successes of Israel and the Jewish people in hi-tech, science, and comedy are but side notes to the elevated spiritual leadership role and responsibility that the Almighty assigned to His people several thousands of years ago, a role that has been reiterated and reaffirmed by the prophets of Israel. All of the news, events, and even the bedlam of the Middle East is leading in that direction, so it's important to understand the news and current events in that religious and national context.

My purpose in writing this book is to clear up at least some of the confusion, and hopefully, to shed some new light on the challenges that we all face in these difficult times.

Acknowledgments

I want to express my appreciation to my pre-press manager/editor, Chaim Mazo, for his steady hand and calm demeanor in seeing this project to fruition.

Special thanks to Ari Sofer, the managing editor at Israel National News (Arutz Sheva, A7) for encouraging me to write my regular blog and providing me with the freedom to do so in my own way.

Thank you, as well, to Rochel Sylvetsky, Op-Eds editor at A7, for originally opening the door for me to write.

Endless thanks are due to my mother, Frieda Rubin, (who completed her seven-year Aliyah last year by finally moving to Israel full-time) for always being a steady source of encouragement, together with my father, Ruby Rubin of blessed memory. It takes enormous wisdom and patience to know how to allow your children to pursue their dreams, even to the other side of the globe. The Creator blessed me with two parents who understood that.

Thank you, as always, to my right-hand man and "Palestinian" Sabra father-in-law, Yossi Stern, who meticulously keeps the SICF paperwork in order during the times when I am busy writing.

Thank you, as well, to the trusted SICF volunteers in other states, in Canada, and in Europe, you know who you are, who selflessly give of their valuable time, helping the children and helping me to get out my message.

Needless to say, words cannot express my appreciation to my holy wife, Lisa, who patiently tolerates and even understands my sudden inspirations to write at what are sometimes very inconvenient times in the life of a family.

Last, but certainly not least, thank you to the Almighty G-d of Israel, who has guided me every step of the way. I am proud to sing His praises.

Israel's News Glossary

Politicians In The News

Abbas, Mahmoud – President of the Palestinian Authority, leader of the Fatah terrorist organization.

Bishara, Azmi – Former Knesset member, passionate Arab anti-Zionist accused of assisting Israel's enemies in wartime, among other treasonous crimes.

Bennett, Naftali – Israeli Economy Minister, leader of the Bayit Yehudi party, previously a self-made millionaire in the high-tech industry.

Diskin, Yuval – Former Israeli Intelligence official, who holds decidedly left-wing views on many issues of national security.

Hotovely, Tzipi – Member of Knesset from the right-wing of the centrist Likud party.

Katsav, Moshe – Former President of Israel, convicted of sexual harassment.

Lapid, Yair – Israeli Finance Minister, leader of the Yesh Atid party, formerly a popular talk show host , author, and journalist.

Liberman, Avigdor – Israeli Foreign Minister, leader of the Yisrael Beytenu party.

Livni, Tzipi – Israeli Minister of Justice, leader of the Hatnuah party, was in charge of peace negotiations with the Palestinian Authority.

Mashal, Khaled – Hamas terrorist organization leader.

Netanyahu, Binyamin (Benjamin) – Prime Minister of Israel, leader of the Likud political party.

Oren, Michael – Former Israeli Ambassador to the United States.

Peres, Shimon – Nonagenarian Israeli politician and former president; as Foreign Minister he was the primary architect of the Oslo Accords and has continued to be a passionate peace process advocate.

Rivlin, Reuven – President of Israel, long-time Likud politician and eighth-generation Israeli.

Yaalon, Moshe – Israeli Defense Minister.

Terms In The News

Areas A, B, C – Division of authority in Judea and Samaria as defined in the Oslo Accords:
Area A – Full Palestinian Authority autonomy.
Area B – Palestinian Authority administrative authority, Israeli security authority.
Area C – Full Israeli authority.

Fatah – The presumed "moderate" Islamic terrorist organization, which is the core of the Palestinian Authority, founded by Yasser Arafat and subsequently led by his successor, Mahmoud Abbas.

Hamas – The Islamic terrorist organization, which is rooted in the Muslim Brotherhood, and has been fighting against Israel from its base in Gaza, but not only.

Hezbollah – Shiite Islamic terrorist organization, based in Lebanon, part of the governing coalition and closely aligned with, and militarily supplied by Iran.

ISIS – The Islamic State in Syria and Iraq – the unabashedly ruthless Islamic terrorist organization; also known as ISIL or IS.

Levy Report – Officially known as the Report on the Legal Status of Building in Judea and Samaria, this 89-page report on the settlements was published on July 9, 2012, after extensive legal and historical research by a three-member committee headed by former Supreme Court Justice Edmund Levy. The report concluded that Israel's presence in Judea and Samaria (the West Bank) cannot accurately be called an occupation and that the Israeli communities in these areas are legal under international law.

MK – Minister of Knesset (Member of the Israeli Parliament).

Oslo Accords – "Peace" agreements secretly negotiated by Israel and the Palestine Liberation Organization and initialed in 1993, starting a process of Israeli withdrawal and/or disengagement from the regions of Judea, Samaria, and Gaza.

Palestinian Authority (PA) – Created by the Oslo Accords as the autonomous quasi-governmental authority in Area A and partially in Area B.

Price Tag Vandalism – Acts of vandalism, presumed by the media to have been carried out by Jews, although in most cases unproven, usually against Islamic or Arab mosques or other institutions, in revenge for terrorist attacks against Jews.

West Bank – the Arab-coined modern term for the contiguous regions of Samaria (north of Jerusalem) and Judea (south of Jerusalem), otherwise known as the historical biblical heartland of Israel.

Major Israeli Political Parties

Bayit Yehudi (Eng: Jewish Home) – a right-wing political party based on the principles of Religious Zionism, which recently united under the broad umbrella of Israelis who respect Jewish tradition and are faithful to the Land of Israel.

Hatnuah – A left-wing political party established by Tzipi Livni with the central purpose of furthering the peace process and preventing nationalistic initiatives.

Kadima – A formerly large, now small and insignificant political party originally started by former Prime Minister Ariel Sharon, Ehud Olmert, and Tzipi Livni for the purpose of carrying out the Israeli withdrawal from Gaza and the destruction of Israeli communities there in 2005.

Labor – A secular, left-wing political party, which for many years was the ruling party in Israel.

Likud – The leading political party in Israel, mostly secular, but considered to be right of center, and most recently led by Prime Minister Binyamin Netanyahu.

Shas – An ultra-Orthodox (Haredi) political party, established with the aim of restoring religious/ethnic pride to the large public of Sephardic Jews. Despite its religious ultra-Orthodox emphasis, it has taken many left of center positions on issues such as the peace process and social welfare.

UTJ (United Torah Judaism) – An ultra-Orthodox (Haredi) political party representing the public of Ashkenazi ultra-Orthodox Jews.

Yesh Atid (Eng: There is a Future) – A secular, left of center political party founded by former journalist Yair Lapid in 2012 that seeks to represent what it considers the center of Israeli society: the secular middle class.

Yisrael Beytenu (Eng: Israel Our Home) – A secular, right of center political party founded by Avigdor Liberman. The party's base has traditionally been Russian-speaking Israelis.

"Nations Will Walk By Your Light
And Kings By The Brilliance Of Your Shine."

Isaiah 60:3

Time For A New Peace Process

The Lord will give strength to His people; the Lord will bless His people with peace.

Psalms 29:11

In light of US President Barack Obama's upcoming visit to Israel, speculation is building as to the main focus that he will be bringing to his meeting with Israeli Prime Minister Binyamin Netanyahu. While pundits on both sides of the ocean are expecting the two leaders to put a positive public spin on their meeting and relationship, the fact is that the tension and disagreements of the past four years are not easily forgotten, not by them and not by their advisors.

It has been reported that Obama is planning to pressure Netanyahu against launching a preemptive attack on Iran's nuclear weapons program, and that may be so, but other reports have begun to emerge that Obama's expected push to renew the sluggish peace process will be even more intense. While the brunt of this pressure will likely be exerted on Netanyahu in private, it will undoubtedly be based once again on the "land for peace" formula, under which Israel is expected to eventually vacate all or most of Judea and Samaria (the "West Bank") and the eastern half of Jerusalem to create a Palestinian state.

It has long been the mantra of the primary peace process promoters that Israel, a country roughly resembling in size the small American state of New Jersey, would need to surrender these areas to bring Israel the elusive peace that it has always sought, even long before its reestablishment as a sovereign nation in 1948. However, after over thirty years of Middle East peace summits and conferences, with millions of dollars wasted on these efforts, resulting in over 1,600 Israeli lives lost in terrorist attacks just in the past twenty years, with thousands of others wounded, perhaps it's time to try something new?

The sad fact is that the peace process has always failed and will continue to fail until we do an abrupt restart and begin to base any future peace process on biblical principles, historical justice, and common sense. Toward this end, I have proposed a new peace plan, which is called Peace For Peace, which does away with the failed land for peace formula and the hopelessly stalled negotiations and offers a unilateral path to peace between Israel and its primarily Arab Muslim neighbors, who it should be clear by now have never abandoned "the stages plan," of using peace negotiations and the land for peace formula to chip away at Israel's concrete assets piece by piece, thereby weakening the Jewish State's resistance. This is an Arab strategy that we have until now foolishly accepted as legitimate, but Peace For Peace changes the rules of the game and stops unrealistically arousing the appetite of the Palestinian wolf. At its core are four key principles:

1. The entire land of Israel is the eternal sovereign inheritance of the Jewish people and no other sovereign nation or quasi-governmental authority can exist within the borders in Israel's possession, which at this time consists of the territory from the Mediterranean Sea to the Jordan River.

2. Israel extends its hand in unconditional peace and cooperation, peace for peace, to all of its neighbors, including those Arabs who live within its borders in Judea and Samaria (the "West Bank").

3.   A path to loyal citizenship in the State of Israel will be offered for all non-citizens of Israel currently living within its borders, including Judea and Samaria. Such a path will include an extensive two-year course in Zionism, Jewish history and good citizenship, culminating in a required oath of loyalty to the Jewish State of Israel, with hand on the Tanach, the Bible of Israel and followed by a 2-3 year commitment of national service to Israel, as performed by all other citizens.

4.   Those who refuse this path of citizenship will be offered a stipend to be resettled in one of the neighboring countries. The option of subsidized transfer will be on the table for one year. After that point, only a small number of non-citizens will be allowed to remain, based on Israel's needs.

As has been revealed in recent demographic studies, Israel need not fear such a scenario. The demographic delusions of Israeli Knesset member Tzipi Livni, who incessantly harps on the demographic threat to Israel that would be caused by the annexation of Judea and Samaria, need not be heeded. As reported extensively by demographic researchers, such as Yoram Ettinger, Israel's growth in Judea and Samaria is now outpacing the Arab growth. In fact, it is the only part of the world in which the demographic struggle opposite the Muslim world is being won.

The time has come for Israel's politicians to learn from past failures and to adopt this new approach to peace – a peace based on biblical principles, historical justice, and common sense.

Who Are Those Refugees?

Only for political and tactical reasons do we speak today about the existence of a Palestinian people, since Arab national interests demand that we posit the existence of a distinct "Palestinian people" to oppose Zionism.

Zahir Muhsein,
PLO executive committee member, 1977

Anyone who travels through Israel sees the many brand new SUV vehicles of UNRWA, the United Nations Relief and Works Agency. Its main activity in Israel is providing assistance to the Arab residents of Judea and Samaria, the so called "West Bank." These residents are commonly known, in UN parlance, as "the Palestinian refugees" along with "millions of others" living in refugee camps in nearby Arab states.

In my book, "Peace For Peace", we debunked the ridiculous notion that there ever was an indigenous sovereign Arab nation called Palestine, so the term Palestinian itself is problematic and historically inaccurate, but since that's the term used by the world, we'll use it here to identify the Arabs of Judea and Samaria and the "millions of refugees" that we are told were driven out of Israel during its 1948 War of Independence.

The United Nations, at its inception, was a beacon of light, a force for peace and hope in a world that had just experienced the horrors of Nazi aggression that left twelve million innocent civilians murdered in cold blood, including six million Jews. Since then, the UN has turned into a bastion of hatred, in which the goal of hurting Israel has become paramount.

In its efforts to harm Israel, the UN specifically declared that hundreds of thousands of Palestinian Arab refugees were driven from Israel between 1946 and 1948. Whether they were driven out as the UN said or whether they left at the urging of the neighboring Arab armies is a matter of some dispute, but one thing is clear – there are only 30,000 of these refugees alive today, a fact that was reaffirmed in a report by the United States Senate Appropriations Committee in May of 2012.

Determined not to lose this issue as a weapon against Israel, the UN redefined its term "Palestinian refugee" to mean not only any Arab who left Israel between the years 1946 and 1948, but all of their descendants as well, thus asserting that there are some five million Palestinian refugees, most of whom have never lived in Israel!

Aside from this gross distortion of history, the United Nations, led by repressive Arab regimes, has ignored the hundreds of thousands of Jewish refugees who were expelled from the Arab nations immediately after the reestablishment of the Jewish State. Unlike the Palestinian Arabs, who are treated as outcasts by their Arab brethren, the 260,000 Jewish refugees out of 800,000, who made it to Israel, were welcomed in by the new Jewish State, which was not yet in a condition to easily absorb them.

None of the Jewish refugees has ever been recognized by the United Nations, nor has the Arab world's responsibility for their displacement been acknowledged. Needless to say, the United Nations has never redefined nor even defined the descendants of the Jewish refugees as refugees deserving of repatriation or even compensation.

Any discussion of the refugee issue in serious peace negotiations must begin with the problem of the Jewish refugees. The Palestinian Authority and the Arab nations have hoodwinked the world into believing their myth of the "millions of Palestinian refugees," giving it a place of honor alongside the myth of the "ancient State of Palestine" that never existed.

The next time they reiterate their lies, let's call their bluff and respond with some truth.

What Israel Can Teach Boston

*"We went to the country (Israel) that's been dealing with the issue for
the past 30 years. We were there to learn from them."*

Paul E. Evans, Boston Police Commissioner

The terror attack in Boston shocked the American people to the core, reminding them that the previous attacks on 9/11 and the subsequent attack at Ft. Hood were not just isolated incidents. Could it be that the attack in Boston is the continuation of a frightening pattern that needs to be confronted?

The nation of Israel has been struggling with such terrorist attacks for decades, at a frequency and proportion that would horrify any free country. Yet, despite the pain and despite the human suffering that comes from such terrorism, there are many key lessons to be learned, and therefore, Israel can teach the United States some fundamental strategies to counter the terrorism and its effects. These lessons can be explained and understood on three levels:

Individual

The trauma of terrorism is deep. After a terror attack, the discussion tends to be about the physical wounds, but the psychological wounds are much deeper, and often are noticed only much later, especially in children. The trauma of terrorism reveals itself in a variety of symptoms, including fear of sleep, exaggerated aggression towards other children, and separation anxiety. Parents should explore the possibility of treatment for their children if these symptoms emerge.

The therapeutic programs supported by the Shiloh Israel Children's Fund in the heartland of Israel use music, art, animals, horses, and multi-sensory safe room therapies to heal the trauma of terrorism. The vast experience gained from these treatments can be applied to American trauma victims as well.

Public

The response of the general public to the trauma of terrorism is critical. Israelis are a resilient people. When there are terror attacks in Israel, people continue to go to work, attend school, and have their leisure and vacation time.

Yes, extra safety precautions are taken. I remember on my first visit to Israel over twenty-five years ago, I visited a department store in Jerusalem. As I entered, a security guard stopped me to check my bag as I entered. Having grown up in New York City, where bags were checked as we left the store, it was surprising to me that in Israel bags were checked at the entrance, because the concern about shoplifting was minimal, while the threat of terrorist bombings was very real.

The safety precautions are accepted lovingly, and we continue to live our lives to the fullest. If we don't, then the terrorists will have won.

Political Leadership

Unlike the current leadership in the United States, which consciously avoids the term "Islamic Terrorism" as unfairly singling out one religious group, most of the political leadership in Israel has always understood that "Jihad" or holy war against non-Muslims is central in the Islamic psyche.

Of course, not all Muslims engage in terrorism, but the potential for such activity is that much greater. Furthermore, Israeli authorities are always cognizant of the formal and informal cooperation between Islamic terrorist groups. These understandings strengthen our strategies as well as our resolve in combating this evil.

An excellent example is Israel's airline security, in which common sense profiling is a central element, even before the passengers reach the airport. Shouldn't a twenty-two-year-old Muslim who has visited Pakistan be subjected to much more rigorous security than a fifth-generation American grandmother from Kansas?

There is also a lesson to be gained from the world of sports. The best defense is a good offense. We have seen that when the Israeli government is on the offensive, aggressively hunting out terrorists and their weapons in the Palestinian Authority autonomous areas, terrorism decreases.

Rather than a scrambling, haphazard approach to battling Islamic terrorism, implementation of the three-level approach that I have outlined above can strengthen the families, the general public, and the law-enforcement authorities in the United States, as well as in the entire free world.

Any delay in doing so is simply irresponsible and will lead to more unnecessary loss of lives.

Can PA Arabs Be
Loyal Citizens Of Israel?

"The test of good citizenship is loyalty to country."

Bainbridge Colby, 19th century American lawyer,
co-founder of the United States Progressive Party

L ikud MK Tzipi Hotovely's citizenship plan for Judea and Samaria Arabs needs to be planned out much more cautiously, in order to protect Israel's interests.

As reported on Arutz Sheva, Deputy Transportation Minister Hotovely is calling on the Israeli government to move towards the annexation of Judea and Samaria, even if it comes with the price of giving citizenship to Arabs residing in these areas. Estimates of the number of Arabs in the area have ranged from 1.5 to 2.4 million.

In the past 35 years, there have been many peace plans, the most recent of which have been based on the "land for peace" formula of Israel surrendering its heartland of Judea and Samaria, as well as eastern Jerusalem to the Palestinian Authority, mainly comprised of the Fatah and Hamas terrorist organizations. With the demonstrated failure of those plans, more and more suggestions are being heard calling for Israel to extend its sovereignty to these regions.

MK Hotovely's proposal to annex all of Judea and Samaria to Israel differs from many pro-annexation proposals in that she calls for the granting of citizenship to the Arab residents. Such a suggestion is certain to bring criticism from both left and right in the political spectrum, with both complaining about the demographic and existential threat that would be caused by the addition of such a large amount of mostly hostile citizens to the Israeli population.

The concern is not misplaced. Even if the most optimistic demographers, such as Yoram Ettinger, who estimate that granting citizenship would bring the total Arab population from the Mediterranean Sea to the Jordan River up to about 35%, are correct, we must understand that the political ramifications of a large Arab minority with increasing demands do not bode well for the State of Israel. On the other hand, declaring Israeli sovereignty without granting citizenship admittedly creates an apartheid-like situation that would greatly heighten the tensions between Israel and the ostensibly friendly nations of the world, including the United States.

Given all of these concerns, I have proposed my Peace For Peace plan, which includes the annexation of Judea and Samaria, as well as a path to loyal citizenship for all residents of the region. Such a path would include an extensive two-year course in Zionism, Jewish history and good citizenship, culminating in a required oath of loyalty to the Jewish State of Israel, and a 2-3 year commitment of national service to Israel, as performed by other citizens. Those residents who accept this offer would in effect be agreeing to become a loyal minority within Israel, much like the Druze community.

The residents of Judea and Samaria who refuse this path to loyal citizenship would be offered a stipend to be resettled in one of the neighboring countries. The option of subsidized transfer would be on the table for one year. After that point, only a small number of non-citizens would be allowed to remain, based solely on Israel's needs.

With the offer on the table, all charges of apartheid would be easily refuted as disingenuous, since the rejection of such an offer would clearly demonstrate the hostility of those particular residents. No country can reasonably be expected to welcome as citizens those who seek its destruction.

This plan to extend Israeli sovereignty to all of Judea and Samaria and to absorb those with the potential to be loyal citizens is a clear, unambiguous plan that can bring historical justice to the region and to all of its inhabitants.

Who Is Minister Of Defense Moshe Yaalon Defending?

"Words empty as the wind are best left unsaid."

Homer
Greek poet, 8th-9th century

All of us who live in Judea and Samaria (the so-called "West Bank", Area C) as well as many other Israeli citizens, are well aware that, along with the resumption of the peace talks in Washington in the past three months, we are witnessing a sharp upturn in the frequency of terrorist attacks on Israeli civilians. These attacks are nothing new, but in the past few weeks, more Jews have been killed or wounded.

Israeli politicians are finally starting to take notice, including Defense Minister Moshe Yaalon, who admitted recently that yes, six terror attacks had taken place in Judea and Samaria in the past month, but added that they were carried out by individuals and did not have an organization such as Fatah or Hamas behind them. He went on to complain that such attacks may have been influenced by "Palestinian incitement."

No doubt there are many residents of Judea and Samaria who are pleased that Yaalon recently visited Hebron, showed some concern, and is aware of the increasing attacks. He even hinted at a strong Israeli response, declaiming, as always, that the IDF "will not rest until we catch the last terrorist involved in these attacks." Having witnessed far too many terror attacks, as well as the usual recurring promises from the leading politicians of a strong response, it is hard for the residents of Israel's biblical heartland not to be skeptical.

More importantly, though, Yaalon's emphasis on the lack of organizational backing is not only disingenuous, but is patently false. It is a well-established fact that up until recently, the Palestinian Authority was bankrolling the terrorist infrastructure, paying salaries to the terrorists and their families. It was reported by Palestinian Media Watch that as of May 2011, the Palestinian Authority was distributing a total of five million dollars monthly to Palestinian terrorist prisoners, continuing and institutionalizing its traditional support for terror, begun during the Yasser Arafat era and expanded under Mahmoud Abbas's leadership. One can safely assume that the payments have continued since.

Is Moshe Yaalon ignorant of this comprehensive network of officially sponsored terror? The problem is not just PA "incitement," but the direct sponsorship and encouragement of terrorist attacks on children and other Israeli civilians. If Minister Yaalon, whose responsibility it is to stop such acts of terrorism, has unquestionable evidence that the PA has stopped such payments to terrorists, he has an obligation as our defense minister to reveal such information. Such a surprising announcement has not been forthcoming.

Barring such a doubtful revelation of a change in PA policy, perhaps it's time for Yaalon to stop making excuses for our "partners in peace," point an accusing finger at Abbas and start defending Israel's citizens.

Too Many Jewishly-Ignorant Would-Be Politicians

"My people are destroyed for lack of knowledge."

Hosea 4:6

Former Shin Bet Chief Yuval Diskin has added his name to a long list of once-distinguished security officials who have become outspoken proponents of expelling Jews and surrendering Jewish land, in anticipation of their impending entry into politics as leftist party candidates.

This strong leftist policy position is usually, we are told, for the noble cause of "peace" and is designed to save Israel from the "unethical" act of taking someone else's land.

Mr. Diskin is no exception to the rule. Speaking at a recent Tel Aviv conference commemorating the ten-year anniversary of the Geneva Initiative, which urged Israel to adopt a two-state solution in negotiations with the Palestinian Authority, Diskin proclaimed that the goal of establishing an independent Palestinian (Arab) state in Judea and Samaria is essential and that the growing number of Jews in those areas are a greater threat to Israel than a nuclear Iran. He went on to call for Israel to become a nation "which prefers the sanctity of its people over the sanctity of its land" and which "does not feel it has to occupy others' land."

One has to wonder which land this former security official for Israel is referring to. Perhaps he was speaking about the faraway land of the pyramids – Egypt. On second thought, could he have been speaking about Saudi Arabia or one of the other Persian Gulf countries? Well, no. In fact, this Israeli security icon was proclaiming that Judea (the region just south of Jerusalem) and Samaria (the region just north of Jerusalem) are Arab lands.

Incredibly, is Diskin telling us that the burial place of the Patriarchs and Matriarchs of Israel (Hebron), that the first city conquered by Joshua upon the entry into the Land of Israel (Jericho), that the childhood home of Samuel the Prophet (Shiloh) and that King David's childhood home (Bethlehem) – that all of these historic Jewish places are "someone else's lands?" Diskin goes on to proclaim that "We must create a new coalition in the Israeli government, one that includes the parties that support peace," while at the same time adding, "My participation here does not hint at any political intentions I might have." Interesting words, but not very convincing.

It seems clear that Diskin is preparing to join a long list of former security officials who, intent on riding on the laurels of their past service, fail to recognize that a political leader of Israel should have a basic knowledge of Jewish history and a commitment to a Jewish destiny that is based on that history. The approximately half a million Jews now living in Judea and Samaria are not a threat to a real, genuine peace. Just the opposite is true. A rapidly growing Jewish population in any part of the Land of Israel is a blessing, a fulfillment of prophecy, and a clear affirmation of our sovereignty in this land.

The world may vociferously condemn us and threaten us, but a true Zionist leader recognizes and affirms the Jewish right to its historic homeland, and yes, acts to unapologetically encourage and actualize the wonderful process of Jewish population growth and settlement in the land.

When it comes to Zionist leadership, Yuval Diskin is clearly not up to the task.

Lapid Is Running Scared

"Politics doesn't make strange bedfellows, marriage does."

Groucho Marx
American comedian

After a dismal showing in a recent popularity survey, Finance Minister Yair Lapid is once again moving left, at least in his public statements, but this time implicitly threatening to abandon his Yesh Atid party's alliance with the religious Zionist Jewish Home (Bayit Yehudi) party.

In a recent Panels poll of Israeli voters rating the job performance of Israel's ministers, Lapid scored dead last among the cabinet's 23 ministers. While it's true that responsible Finance Ministers tend to do poorly in these surveys because of the frequent need to impose unpopular spending cuts to reduce the deficit, the extreme result of that survey may be seen as surprising and frightening for Lapid, especially given the popularity of Yesh Atid in last year's election.

It seems that the poll results did, indeed, come as a shock to Lapid, and therefore, his response has been quick and very public on the political front. The issue of the ongoing negotiations between Israel and the Palestinian Authority, commonly referred to as peace talks, has been increasingly contentious in the coalition, but hasn't yet torn it apart.

In a clear signal to his many disappointed left-wing voters, Lapid took action to stem his sharp popularity decline. Speaking at the Globes Israel Business conference in Tel Aviv, Lapid, in a clear and unprecedented swipe at his Jewish Home partner, which has led the opposition to a Palestinian state, said that the coalition must be aware that Yesh Atid "will see to it that those who seek to undermine the negotiations will pay a heavy political price." Time flies when you're having political fun as strange bedfellows, but we should remember that it's only been less than a year since Lapid and Jewish Home leader Naftali Bennett established their bold political alliance, which successfully prevented Prime Minister Netanyahu from leaving either party out of the coalition in formation.

The strategic alliance, despite the fierce criticism that it aroused from both the Haredi (ultra-Orthodox) and most of the strongly secular parties, clearly was a brilliant out of the box maneuver by both leaders. The ability on the part of both Bennett and Lapid to transcend clear political differences on religion and state, as well as on the pivotal issue of whether to create an independent Palestinian state in Judea and Samaria and Jerusalem, left the other political parties flabbergasted, yet helpless to respond.

Less than one year later, the tides seem to be shifting. In recent days, we have seen Jewish Home joining forces with Avigdor Liberman's center-right Yisrael Beytenu party to block a Yesh Atid-sponsored civil union/gay marriage law, an action which has greatly angered some of the more left-leaning Yesh Atid Knesset members, possibly even including Lapid himself.

After an attempt by Jewish Home to weld together a compromise wording – rejecting recognition of gay marriage, but allowing a form of civil union for everyone else – was rejected by Yesh Atid, the Jewish Home cooperated with Yisrael Beytenu to torpedo the bill.

Lapid's latest public statement, implicitly threatening to break up the current coalition by encouraging the replacement of Jewish Home with one of the left-wing Opposition parties, could be the beginning of the end for the Bennett-Lapid alliance, but may also be a harbinger of new political alliances in formation.

Whether Lapid's threat represents political revenge or is simply a desperate response by a scared politician concerned about losing his voter base, we should not be surprised if the Jewish Home starts exploring a different strategic direction.

Michael Oren's Peace Plan:
Salvation Or Suicide?

"But in the end one needs more courage to live than to kill himself."

Albert Camus
French-Algerian philosopher

C an another unilateral plan, another "disengagement," be good for Israel? If so, what kind?
Former Israeli Ambassador to the United States Michael Oren has announced his support for a unilateral withdrawal from Judea and Samaria, on the condition that the current peace negotiations with the Palestinian Authority aren't successful. He is justifying his position by citing the threats from the PA leadership to go back to the United Nations with their statehood bid. In a curious nod to the failures of the unilateral withdrawal from Gaza in 2005, Oren goes on to qualify his stand by emphasizing that this time, Israel should protect its security interests.

One has to wonder what planet Mr. Oren is living on when he speaks of protecting security interests. Handing over the strategic Judea-Samaria mountain ridge to the Fatah- and soon to be Hamas-led PA is nothing short of the abandonment of Israel's security interests, bordering on national suicide.

I hereby challenge Mr. Oren to answer the following questions:

1.   As a nation that cares about its citizens and hopefully

has learned the sad lessons of the hasty retreats from Lebanon and Gaza, can we afford to take the risk of surrendering the Western Samarian hills with their bird's-eye view of Israel's only international airport? Does the esteemed former ambassador really want to turn the strategic hilltop communities of Samaria into missile launching pads – learn the lessons of Gaza – for Hamas and Islamic Jihad? Once the State of Palestine is established and unilaterally given control and sovereignty over those high points, how does he plan to stop the missiles from flying?

2. Furthermore, once we withdraw, how does he intend to prevent the reestablishment of bomb and weapon factories in the cities of Ramallah, Shechem, Kalkilya, and all the others which, unlike Gaza, are in close proximity to Israel's largest cities? This is not some theoretical guessing game in the halls of academia. We have been there, done that and it does not bear repeating. Such a plan endangers Israel's very existence as a sovereign nation in its land and it would be the epitome of suicidal naiveté to implement such a plan of retreat.

As I propose in the last chapter of my most recent book, "Peace for Peace: Israel in the New Middle East", a unilateral peace plan doesn't have to include Israeli retreat. We are a vibrant, growing nation in which the Jewish rate of population growth is increasing, while the Arab growth rate is dropping. That doesn't mean we can't reach out to the Arab residents of Judea and Samaria who choose to accept Israeli sovereignty. We can offer a challenging path to loyal citizenship for all non-citizen residents that could even include a comprehensive course in Zionist history and civics, culminating in national service and an oath of loyalty with hand on the Bible, Tanach.

All those who would reject this option would be given a stipend, with a limited amount of time to leave peacefully for another country.

The foolish land-for-peace formula, otherwise known as the two-state solution, whether bilateral or unilateral, is a recipe for the destruction of Israel. Protecting our national interests means safeguarding our territory, protecting the low points, protecting the airports, and protecting all of the citizens of our nation. Any other approach, including Oren's plan, is simply irresponsible.

Confronting The Apartheid Canard

"A propensity to delay difficult and weighty decisions has been hurting our country."

Yoshihiko Noda
Former Prime Minister of Japan

There has been a great deal of fuss about US Secretary of State John Kerry's comments implying that Israel risks becoming an "apartheid state" if a deal is not reached with the Palestinian Authority. While the comments sparked outraged comments from Israeli government ministers such as Transportation Minister Yisrael Katz, the question needs to be asked honestly, "Does Israel risk becoming an apartheid state if it fails to address the question of non-citizen status for the Arab residents of the disputed regions of Judea and Samaria (the 'West Bank')"?

While there is no doubt that Israel recaptured these areas in a defensive war in 1967, the very indecisive way in which repeated Israeli governments have failed to address the "apartheid genie" has opened the door to these charges, however unjustified. As long as the issue is ignored, the charges will only intensify.

Undoubtedly, the issue will fester for now, at least until Israel either surrenders the areas or declares its sovereignty over the Land of Israel from the Mediterranean Sea to the Jordan River. Nonetheless, despite the new unity pact between Hamas and Fatah in the Palestinian Authority, there are but a few voices in the Knesset calling for an Israeli declaration of sovereignty over Judea and Samaria, and if so, only over

Area C, the 60% of Judea and Samaria (the so-called "West Bank"), in which most of its approximately 350,000 Jewish citizens live.

Those individuals, such as Minister Naftali Bennett (Bayit Yehudi), continue to ignore the difficult issue of defining appropriate conditions, on the road to loyal citizenship, if possible, for the Arab residents of these areas. To declare sovereignty without offering citizenship to the Arab residents indeed adds fuel to the accusations of apartheid, although there are many other places in the world where inhabitants of countries are not granted citizenship. To grant unconditional citizenship would be the epitome of national suicide, in effect giving legitimacy to those who are hostile to our very existence in our historic homeland.

The solution to this dilemma can be found in my peace proposal, which is a unilateral plan entitled "Peace For Peace." According to this plan, full Israeli sovereignty would immediately be declared over all of the areas in our possession from the Mediterranean Sea to the Jordan River. Simultaneously, a "path to loyal citizenship," would be offered to all the residents of Judea and Samaria, which would include the following mandatory steps by all applicants:

1. Completion of a two-year course in Zionism, Jewish history and good citizenship.

2. Commitment to perform two to three years of appropriate national service like all Israeli citizens.

3. An oath of loyalty, with hand on Tanach – the Hebrew Bible – to the Jewish State of Israel.

Those who complete these obligations successfully would be welcomed as full citizens of Israel. Those who refuse would be given a stipend with a limited period of time to relocate to a different country.

The "apartheid state" charge would be proven false by this generous offer. Every country has the right to set an appropriate standard by which it screens and perhaps accepts new citizens and this would be no exception, and the door to full rights and responsibilities would be open to those who are worthy. This is quite standard in the civilized world.

Especially in a sensitive situation like ours, in which the Arab residents have often been hostile towards the State of Israel, it is the utmost in responsible caution to require that all potential citizens prove their sincerity in that quest. I strongly recommend that Israel's leaders end the vacillating, ambiguous posture and boldly adopt this creative plan which will both insure Israel's survival and its moral stature.

Obsession Against "Settlers"

"Do you know what we call opinion in the absence of evidence? We call it prejudice."

Michael Crichton
American author, State of Fear

Justice Minister Tzipi Livni is on a new rampage. Just a few short weeks after the bitter failure of her latest passion – the "peace process" negotiations with the Fatah-Hamas terrorists that comprise the Palestinian Authority – she is once again adhering to the motto that the best defense is a good offense.

Citing the few incidents of "price tag" vandalism of army vehicles, allegedly carried out by some fringe hotheads in Judea and Samaria, Livni has now gone on record slandering all of the hundreds of thousands of idealistic law-abiding Jews living in these areas, as well as their supporters.

In defense of her blatant failure as the Israeli government's chief peace negotiator, Livni went on the offensive, blasting "those who rightly denounce 'Price Tag,' but will do everything to find every loophole and political weakness in order to keep us from a diplomatic solution, and do so while mortally wounding the world's relations with Israel." She goes on to say that "What began as love of the land has now partly turned into a wild west sown with hatred toward Arabs and toward the rule of law and its representatives – be they dressed in judges' robes, police uniforms or IDF uniforms."

To plaster with a broad brush an entire segment of the

population for the alleged actions of a few individuals is not only the height of chutzpah, but is outright bigotry towards some of the most dedicated Zionists in Israel. Does she not know that from this population on which she so vehemently spews her invective, have come a greatly disproportionate number of officers in the IDF? Is the esteemed Justice Minister unaware that the heartland communities have suffered the vast brunt of shooting and firebomb attacks perpetrated by her beloved "peace partners?"

Such bigotry is shameful, whatever its target. Given the increase in rapes and other attacks in the streets of Ms. Livni's hometown of Tel Aviv, would it be proper to criticize all the residents of Tel Aviv with hatred towards women, towards innocent pedestrians, towards joggers, and other victims of such attacks? Perhaps the Justice Minister herself should be investigated for such street crimes in her city?

Let's call a spade a spade. The peace process has failed because for the past 50 years, we as a nation have been banging our proverbial "land for peace" heads against the wall in a wild messianic pursuit of a new Middle East, of which Tzipi Livni is a prominent wild-eyed proponent. Since the expulsion from Gaza and northern Samaria in 2005, this mystical promoter of "peace at all costs" has staked her political career on the suicidal concept of Israeli surrender of its most strategic and historic lands to an armed band of Islamic terrorists.

Rather than walking back home to north Tel Aviv with her head bowed in shame, as she should if she has any measure of humility in her character, she continues to attack those who have been proven right by her latest failure.

Perhaps this dangerous politician needs to be sent home before she does more damage to her country's vital interests and before more lives are lost in her wild pursuit of a false peace with those who wish to destroy us.

The Bibi And Ruby Show

"Look around. There are no enemies here. There's just good, old-fashioned rivalry."

Bob Wells
American athlete

For weeks now, political analysts have been having a field day watching the political scrambles as Prime Minister Binyamin (Bibi) Netanyahu has been doing everything in his power to avoid supporting MK and former Knesset Speaker Reuven (Ruby) Rivlin (Likud) as President.

The intensive attempts to end the position of President altogether or at least to postpone this election, now scheduled for early in June, have ostensibly been behind the scenes, but in actuality, they have been very much in the public eye, and frankly, it's been quite an embarrassing display of political maneuvering.

This has been followed by intensive meetings held by the PM with alternative possible candidates such as Minister Silvan Shalom (Likud) and rumors abound that Netanyahu may even support former Knesset Speaker Dalia Itzik, despite the fact that she was an MK from the left of center Labor and Kadima parties and was never in Netanyahu's Likud. In short, anyone but Rivlin.

Certainly a strong argument can be made for completely ditching the post of President, once and for all. Can't the presidential functions of greeting foreign dignitaries, granting clemency, and serving as a conscience for the nation be fulfilled by others? Furthermore, after the Katsav fiasco and after the last several years with "Mr. Peace Process" Peres abusing the position for partisan political purposes, wouldn't it be wise to save millions of taxpayer funds by disposing of the position?

The short answer is yes, but such a change can't be ethically enacted just before an election. To do so would be correctly perceived as political opportunism, especially if Netanyahu is the initiator.

This leaves Israel's Prime Minister with only one sensible option – to act as a statesman rather than a petty politician. Everyone in the Knesset, not to mention the Likud and other members of the ruling coalition, knows that Ruby Rivlin is the leading candidate. He is well-liked as a person and clearly gained great respect for his dignity and fairness as Knesset Speaker, with those attributes recognized across the political spectrum.

The time has come for Ruby and Bibi to meet for a cup of coffee, if not for lunch, and to work out whatever personality differences or conflicts have led them to this dilemma. Such a simple solution should reasonably be expected of any two adults in a position of responsibility, but all the more so for the Prime Minister and the potential President of Israel.

It would also be a positive example for every citizen of Israel. And that's good politics.

Middle East Advice For America

"And he shall be a wild-ass of a man; his hand against everyone and everyone's hand against him ..."

Genesis 16:12

While Israel has been absorbed in the Palestinian terrorist kidnapping of three Israeli teenagers, including one who is also an American citizen, the attention in the United States has been focused on the crisis in Iraq. A public debate has been raging in the US over the best way of responding to the ISIS offensive, in which the well-armed and financed Sunni Muslim militia is storming western Iraq on its way to Baghdad.

This is a debate that seems to cross party lines, with leading Republicans such as former Vice-President Dick Cheney advocating strong and decisive American military action on behalf of the embattled predominantly Shiite government of Prime Minister Nouri al-Maliki, and others such as Senator Rand Paul calling for cautious analysis before throwing American troops and/or weapons into another failed overseas adventure.

Meanwhile, President Barack Obama seems to be indecisive, but leaning towards a more robust American response to stop the ISIS surge, and therefore, has sent Secretary of State John Kerry to Baghdad for emergency consultations to attempt to stabilize the Maliki government and to increase cooperation between the dominant Shiite faction and the increasingly marginalized and alienated Sunni and Kurdish components of his current government.

The problem with all of these approaches, as well as the problem with the American involvement in Iraq in general, is that they ignore the concept of self-interest, which, at least in the Middle East, is everything. Rather than reflexively getting involved and embroiled in an internal Islamic, ethnic rivalry, or, conversely, avoiding all involvement, it behooves a wise leader to examine who is a potential friend and who is an enemy.

Everyone seems to agree that the al-Qaeda-linked ISIS is no friend of the West, but it has been reported that they are receiving substantial financial support from (supposed American allies) Saudi Arabia and Qatar, who as Sunnis, are siding with their brethren.

Maliki, who is a Shiite Muslim, has minimally cooperated with the United States just to maintain his position, but the Shiite Muslims in the Middle East, including in Iraq, are primarily aligned with Iran, which is feverishly preparing ballistic missiles that can reach the United States with the nuclear bombs that they hope to soon possess. Yes, the Iranians are sworn to Israel's destruction, but such long-range missiles aren't needed to reach Israel.

The only one of the three dominant forces in Iraq that is relatively pro-Western is the Kurds, a fairly cohesive group that is solidly entrenched in Northeastern Iraq in a region that is rich in oil wealth. The Shiites and Sunnis are both Jihadist and seek the destruction of Judeo-Christian civilization, so what is the purpose of reengaging and sending troops or any kind of support to either of them? Let the Sunnis and Shiites fight it out – and may they both lose. As they are both enemies of the United States, the West, and Israel, it cannot hurt to have them fighting each other.

It's certainly not "politically correct" to say so, but the bloody Islamic ethnic standoff in Syria has succeeded in weakening both the Sunni rebels and Assad's Alawite/Shiite government. In short, two enemies of the West are fighting each other and that's good. The interests of the free world dictate letting the civil war continue and quietly encouraging a stand-off.

The Syrian model can be learned from. A long-term Shiite-Sunni war in Iraq can only be beneficial to the West's war on Islamic terrorism. It would be greatly advisable to covertly enable and encourage such a standoff, while providing political and passive military support to the Kurds in their quest for stability, and eventual independence. They are the only ones in Iraq that can reasonably be expected to protect Western interests in exchange for such assistance, so they should be supported.

As for the Shiite-Sunni Jihadist battlefields? Disengage.

Rand Paul And Israel: AIPAC Fails The Test

"Cleave ever to the sunnier side of doubt."

Lord Alfred Tennyson
19th century British Poet

There has been much skepticism about the pro-Israel credentials of Sen. Rand Paul (R-KY), a likely candidate for US President in 2016. This is mainly due to the anti-Israel image of his father Sen. Ron Paul, who once accused Israel of putting the so-called Palestinians in something resembling a "concentration camp" in Gaza. While I was in the forefront of those criticizing Paul the father for his stance on Israel, it seems blatantly unfair to criticize the son for the misguided statements of the father.

In light of the above qualification, I want to strongly compliment Sen. Rand Paul on his proposed bill to halt all American aid to the Palestinian Authority until the Hamas-Fatah unity coalition recognizes Israel's right to exist as the nation-state of the Jewish People. This is a perfectly sensible and moderate bill to stop assistance to a quasi-governmental authority that supports terrorism.

Surprisingly, AIPAC (The America-Israel Public Affairs Committee) – generally perceived as a strongly pro-Israel lobbying group – has reportedly been making a strong effort to torpedo this bill. If this is accurate, it is an outrage.

Could it possibly be due to an anti-Republican bias in AIPAC? Could it be that AIPAC is afraid of hurting the illusory peace process or making waves with the White House? Is it unreasonable for supporters of Israel to expect a response and explanation from the movers and shakers in AIPAC?

Clarification Is Always Good

"The unseen enemy is always the most fearsome."

George R. R. Martin
American novelist

Fatah-Tanzim terrorist Marwan Barghouti, who is serving five life sentences in an Israeli prison for his leading role in planning suicide terror attacks, has welcomed the Hamas-Fatah unity pact and stressed that there can never be a peace agreement with Israel unless what he calls "Palestinian refugees" are allowed to return to their homes.

Unlike the Israeli officials who are embarrassed by these statements, which hurt their hopes of crowning this vile terrorist as Mahmoud Abbas's successor, I say that it's always good to know what people really think, not what the spin doctors tell us to further their sacred agenda of so-called peace. Clarification is always good.

The 30,000 "Palestinian" refugees (those who are still alive), who fled their homes willingly in 1948 should be given the right of return. Yes, they are welcome to return to the Arabian peninsula from where most of them came in the early part of the 20th century. They can take their descendants with them. It's time to start talking about the refugees that the UN has always ignored – the hundreds of thousands of Jews who were forced out of the Arab countries after the State of Israel was reestablished in 1948.

"You Stole Palestine!"

"We've had an invented Palestinian people who are in fact Arabs and who were historically part of the Arab community. And they had a chance to go many places, and for a variety of political reasons we have sustained this war against Israel ..."

Newt Gingrich
Former Speaker, US House of Representatives

In the course of my speaking tours outside of Israel, and even on my Facebook page, I am often confronted by the haters of Israel who accuse me of stealing a fictional country called Palestine. While I could feel for them if they had a legitimate gripe, it seems a bit dishonest to reclaim a country that never existed.

I hereby challenge all supporters of "Palestine" to answer the following questions:

1. In what year was that ancient nation called Palestine established?

2. Who was the first leader of that country and in what year did he take office?

3. What was the monetary currency of that ancient country called Palestine?

Sadly for the haters of Israel, no one can answer those questions because there never was an ancient country called Palestine. However there was a Kingdom of Israel, led by King David and King Solomon, among others.

The above three questions should be asked and asked

again to those fools who repeatedly charge Israel with "stealing Palestinian land." No honest person can answer those questions because there never was a sovereign nation called Palestine, certainly not one consisting of Arabs or Arab Muslims.

Yes, the conquering Romans 2,000 years ago had changed the name from Judea or Israel to Palestina, naming the land after the Philistines, the long-time enemies of Israel, but there were no Arabs to speak of here.

As for Muslims, they didn't even exist until some 600 years later. So much for the nonsensical and historically false charge of "stealing Palestinian land."

Benedict And Tzipi:
A Fair Comparison?

"The pacifist is as surely a traitor to his country and to humanity as is the most brutal wrongdoer."

Theodore Roosevelt
American President

B enedict Arnold was a general who originally fought for the American Continental Army but defected to the British Army, thereby earning for himself the dishonorable title as the prototype traitor.

While not actually defecting to a foreign army, Justice Minister Tzipi Livni's recent pow-wow with Palestinian Authority President Mahmoud Abbas has now been revealed to be a clear act of disobedience to the orders of Prime Minister Binyamin Netanyahu. According to the latest reports, Netanyahu clearly told her that to meet with the leader of the Fatah-Hamas unity government would be in direct contradiction to the recent Israeli Cabinet decision to break off all contact with the PA leadership, which has chosen partnership with Hamas over peace with Israel.

To meet with the leader of the enemy that has been responsible for the murder and wounding of thousands of Israelis, and to do so in violation of the Cabinet decision seems to be a treasonous act. Are we afraid to say the word "traitor" when a leading coalition politician shows a strange passion for cavorting with the enemy?

The Political Pope Arrives In Israel

"The evil that is in the world almost always comes of ignorance, and good intentions may do as much harm as malevolence if they lack understanding."

Albert Camus
French-Algerian philosopher

P ope Francis is in Israel, ostensibly with a message of peace, as opposed to politics, but is it really so? His actions so far seem to speak otherwise.

The Pope's pointed reference to "the State of Palestine" and his decision to fly directly from Jordan to Bethlehem, thereby skipping over Israeli territory, was interpreted by many as symbolic political support for the creation of an independent Palestinian state. As his day continued, he made a stop at the security wall that separates Jerusalem from Bethlehem, the defensive barrier that Israel had built about ten years ago to protect Israel's capital from Islamic suicide bombers. In what could only be understood as a blatant political act, the Pope bowed his head and prayed in front of a bold graffiti display, which proclaimed, "Free Palestine!" If it was justice that the Pope was seeking in Bethlehem, he could have easily made reference to the ongoing persecution and violent intimidation of local Christians at the hands of the Palestinian Authority, which has rapidly shrunk the once robust 80% Christian population down to less than 15%. Could the Pope have said a prayer for the suffering of these Christian victims of Islamic intolerance?

Perhaps the most righteous prayer could have been

dedicated to the memory of the thousands of Israeli victims of Islamic terrorism emanating from "Palestinian" controlled cities like Bethlehem. It's sad but true, that the Vatican doesn't have a stellar record when it comes to protecting its own children in its child abuse scandals, so perhaps we shouldn't be surprised by its lack of recognition for the suffering of Jewish children who've been victimized by the Fatah terror group led by "man of peace" Mahmoud Abbas.

The message emanating from this Pope at the start of his trip was not peace. It was anti-Israel politics. There is nothing holy about collusion between Abbas, the primary employer of Islamic terrorists, and the Pope, a seemingly sincere religious leader that is believed to represent over a billion people. However, true holiness and true peace cannot be genuine, if it's not based on the accurate recognition of evil and on the spreading of goodness. True prayer needs to reflect that dual reality, and hopefully Pope Francis will have the humility to learn that lesson as his relationship with Israel continues to develop. Otherwise, it's all just a media show of the worst kind.

The Right-Wing In Europe: Neo-Nazis?

"How dreadful are the curses which Muhammedanism lays on its votaries! Besides the fanatical frenzy, which is as dangerous in a man as hydrophobia in a dog, there is this fearful fatalistic apathy ... Far from being moribund, Muhammedanism is a militant and proselytizing faith."

Winston Churchill, 1899

The continuing rise of the various right-wing parties in Europe, often derisively dismissed as "far-right" or even "neo-Nazi" by their opponents, has been a clear trend for a number of years now and is certainly a force to be reckoned with. They have many harsh critics, including some leaders in the European Jewish community, but are those critics going too far in their name-calling?

Such blanket criticism ignores the many positive aspects of this primarily anti-EU and anti-immigration movement, which is justifiably concerned about the dangerous growth of Islamic populations, Islamic influence, and yes, Islamic terrorism throughout Europe. Recent years have also seen a sharp increase in crimes such as rapes and Muslim-initiated anti-Semitic attacks in European cities. This has been accompanied by demands for Sharia law – that oppressive Islamic law that would, for example, stifle any public expression of religious observance other than Islam, would legalize wife-beating, and would require cutting off the hands of shoplifters.

During a recent speaking tour in Sweden, I had the privilege of meeting in the Parliament with several leaders of the Swedish Democrats, the one party in Sweden that is active in attempting to combat the Islamic demographic threat to this formerly peaceful, friendly country. We engaged in serious dialogue about the issues confronting our two countries and I was impressed by their deep concern for their now internally embattled country's future. Even more so, I was struck by their sincere desire to understand the importance and the benefit of standing with a confident Israel that has returned to its biblical, historic heartland, as well as the importance of learning about the heritage and the central cultural symbols of the Jewish people – such as kashrut and circumcision – which are increasingly under attack in today's Europe. Such genuine interest in achieving understanding and cooperation would certainly not be expressed by neo-Nazis. Positive trends like this should be welcomed and encouraged.

Yes, there is a wide range of opinion in the various right-wing parties in the European countries as it concerns their attitudes towards Israel and the Jewish people, from strongly pro-Israel to anti-Semitic, but distinctions need to be made in developing a plan for contending with these trends. In any event, the real and consistent threat to Israel comes from the European Left, which has repeatedly proven its dangerous anti-Israel leanings by shamelessly cavorting with the Islamic ideologues and other haters of Israel.

The very real concerns that have fueled the rise of the Right in Europe will not disappear and will only grow in the coming years. Perhaps it's time that we Israelis put aside the old right-left stereotypes concerning our relations with the different movements in Europe and start focusing on building constructive relationships, to honestly confront the issues at hand. Once we make this basic conceptual shift, then we can take serious steps to steer the entire European ship to a positive relationship with Israel and the Jewish people. If that happens, it will be good for Europe, as well.

Liberman, Rivlin, And
The Land Of Israel

"So the Lord gave Israel the entire land that He had sworn to give their forefathers; they inherited it and dwelled in it."

Joshua 21:41

Foreign Minister Avigdor Liberman has announced that he cannot "in principle" support former Knesset Speaker Reuven (Ruby) Rivlin in the presidential race because of the latter's past opposition to stripping former MK Azmi Bishara of his pension rights. Bishara had fled the country to avoid facing charges of treason.

Bishara allegedly received several hundred thousand dollars from Hezbollah in exchange for delivering intelligence information, during the 2006 Second Lebanon War. He was also in touch with intelligence agents from other unnamed countries.

"I always try to be clear," Liberman said. "I do not run away from reality and I provide answers. I made clear that I would not vote for Rivlin. I did not support him when he ran against Peres. I told him that I would not support him, even if he was the favorite."

Rivlin had claimed that Bishara was innocent until proven guilty and that he couldn't support removing the rights of an MK until a proper investigation and legal process was completed. Liberman now charges that Rivlin was actually currying favor with Arab MKs for his future presidential run.

Whatever one's opinion of Rivlin's judgment on the Bishara case, Liberman should not be turning this one issue into a vendetta against Rivlin. Liberman was already terribly mistaken in supporting Mr. "Peace Process" Peres in the previous election. Two central questions need to be asked of the esteemed FM:

1. Why did Liberman support Peres, who has always supported Arab sovereignty in the areas that Israel liberated in 1967 – instead of Rivlin – who has always been a staunch opponent of Israeli withdrawals from the Land of Israel?

2. Why does Liberman – even in these days of Hamas-Fatah unity – continue to advocate and actively promote his "land exchange" plan for Israeli withdrawal from large parts of the Land of Israel, including even parts of Jerusalem?

The great American President Theodore Roosevelt was known for his expression "Speak softly and carry a big stick." Liberman has turned this expression on its head. Shouting at Arab MKs may be justifiable in some cases and Rivlin may have been wrong about the Bishara case, but Liberman needs to understand that sound bites are not a substitute for substantive policy and faithfulness to the Land of Israel.

Aside from being recognized by all as a mensch and a man of integrity, Reuven Rivlin has been a consistent supporter of the complete Land of Israel under Israeli sovereignty. Liberman has not. After the peace process politics of Peres have almost turned the presidency into a pro-withdrawal advocacy position, it's time for a change. Liberman should think again – To vote for another withdrawal candidate would be a big mistake and a true betrayal of the country.

Bibi And Building:
The Buck Stops Here

"They shall dwell securely in it, and they shall build houses and plant vineyards. They shall dwell securely, when I execute judgments upon all their neighbors who have treated them with contempt. Then they will know that I am the Lord their God."

Ezekiel 28:26

In which unilateral direction is Bibi going in response to Hamas-Fatah unity? Towards Israeli sovereignty or towards Israeli withdrawal? To understand the direction, one needs to examine Prime Minister Netanyahu's actions, but also his statements, both of which reveal a disturbing lack of faithfulness to the principle of Israeli sovereignty in the Land of Israel.

At a recent meeting of the Knesset Foreign Affairs and Defense Committee, Netanyahu pointedly remarked, "I don't want one state from the (Mediterranean) Sea to the Jordan (River) ... we must separate from the Palestinians." This weak statement is noticeably similar to those previously made by former prime ministers Ehud Barak and Ariel Sharon, who both strongly advocated Israeli withdrawal.

Since Prime Minister Netanyahu was elected, and even since the unity announcement, almost all of the Jewish building permitted in Judea and Samaria has been close to the green line, the imaginary pre-1967 border. Meanwhile, Arab building has continued unabated, even including Rawabi, a brand new Arab city in the heart of Samaria. Rawabi is being rapidly and massively built with Netanyahu's blessing and support. At the same time, not one new Jewish community with permanent housing has been established in Samaria since Netanyahu was elected, and in those that have existed for many years, the demand for housing is much greater than the supply. The reason? Few permits are being granted for building projects in Jewish communities, other than those close to the green line or in the largest communities.

American President Harry Truman was known for his motto, "The Buck Stops Here," meaning that the leader of a country has to take responsibility for the government's actions, or in this case, inaction.

It's time that we stop blaming defense ministers, the media, or Tzipi Livni for Prime Minister Netanyahu's anti-Zionist policies in Judea and Samaria. Once Netanyahu decides in his heart that Jews have the right to live in all parts of the Land of Israel, the next steps will be easy. The Levy Report asserting our right to the land will be approved, the building permits will flow, and the world will be reduced to condemnations and threats, but a proud Zionist vision will be implemented. I wish that we could rely on the PM's Jewish heart, as well as his head, to draw the proper conclusions, but at least at this time, it seems very clear that only heavy coalition pressure from the right will steer Bibi in this direction.

Does Israel Need
A Jewish Republican In Congress?

"There continue to be stark partisan differences in Middle East sympathies. Conservative Republicans maintain strong support for Israel with fully 75% saying they sympathize with Israel compared with just 2% who sympathize with the Palestinians. By contrast, liberal Democrats are much more divided: 33% sympathize more with Israel, 22% with the Palestinians."

Conclusions of Pew Research Center Poll, December 2013

After the resounding defeat of US Republican Eric Cantor after seven terms in Congress, there are now no Jewish Republicans remaining in Congress. Is that a problem for the GOP? More importantly, is that a problem for Israel?

We can certainly expect the Democrats to pounce on this vacuum to score political points. Undoubtedly, they will be boasting about their pro-Israel credentials in the coming elections and many Jews will be easily persuaded by the ethnic numbers.

However, we who actually live in tiny Israel can't afford to play that game. We remember all too well the forced building freezes, the forced terrorist releases, the implied boycott threats, and the apartheid charges of the DC Democratic triumvirate of Obama, Clinton, and Kerry. We also remember the firm support emanating from the right side of the aisle, which even has recently begun to question the flawed idea of creating a "Palestinian" state in Israel's biblical, historical heartland. Some leading Republicans have also started doubting the latest gospel – the recently invented concept of an "indigenous" Palestinian people. Furthermore, they have been outspoken in their skepticism about the dangerous American negotiations with soon-to-be nuclear Iran.

Whether these Republicans have been urged on by the strong Christian Zionist presence in the GOP or simply by a basic instinct for what is true justice, many of these pro-Israel Republicans have put their knee-jerk liberal Jewish colleagues on the other side of the aisle to shame in their strong support for the Jewish State in its ongoing existential struggle.

Would it be useful for Republicans to seek out and encourage a flock of good Republican Jewish candidates? Yes, of course, but that may be a daunting task, given the rightward drift in the GOP, along with the dogmatic social liberalism of much of American Jewry, with the notable exception of those who identify as Orthodox. Nonetheless, we here in Israel will continue to judge our overseas friends by their actions. Those who support a thriving, growing Jewish State in its ancient borders are our true allies, even if they're not Jewish. Yes, a little tribal loyalty and tribal pride can be a nice thing, but I prefer survival.

The Iraqi Paradox,
Or What Is An Islamist?

"Whether most Muslims are peaceable is irrelevant. The fact is that fanatics rule Islam now and act out what the Koran truly says ... maul, march, and murder every Infidel if they won't convert!"

Gary Patton, Canadian author

Several years ago, I was on a radio show in the United States, shortly after the release of my book "The Islamic Tsunami: Israel and America in the Age of Obama" and I started to speak about the Islamic threat to the free world. At that moment, my nervous host jumped in and pointed out that I was speaking about "Radical Islam," not Islam itself. To this I politely corrected him, saying that I was indeed speaking about Islam itself, the core of which is radical.

Nonetheless, despite the philosophy of Jihad, or holy war against "unbelievers," which has become the central guiding light in Islamic practice today, commentators in the media are fearful of confronting the danger of this ideology that has clearly become the "religious" justification for terrorism. The fact is that elaborate games of semantic gymnastics are created to avoid criticizing the core doctrines of Islam.

For some years now, we have been hearing the term "Islamist" (as opposed to Islamic or Muslim) to describe the Jihadists that are supposedly "the fringe" elements of Islam. The absurdity of the term should have been apparent in the recent reports that Iran is sending its soldiers to "fight the Islamists" in Iraq. Wait a second – Aren't we always told that the Iranians are the world's biggest supporters of Jihad? So why aren't they called Islamists?

Oh, now I understand. It must be that the Iranian Shiite Muslims are the moderate core of Islam!!!

In all seriousness, false distinctions such as Islamic vs. Islamist will not change the facts. Most practicing Muslims believe in Jihad, even if not actively engaged in it or supporting it. The Shiite Muslim Ayatollahs in Iran are not a moderate force fighting "Islamists." Indeed, Shiite Muslims who believe in and are active in Jihad are being sent to Iraq to fight against Sunni Muslims who believe in and are active in Jihad. Both are fighting to see who will get to lead the Islamic Tsunami against Israel and against the West. Other than the Kurds, who are the most pro-Western force in Iraq, there are no good guys there – just wild-eyed Jihadist Muslims – sworn to eliminate (in their words) first the Saturday people and then the Sunday people.

But at least for now they're fighting each other.

Enough Empty Threats!

"Empty threats are often worse than saying nothing at all. It's like leading from behind. Eventually, no one thinks you're leading at all. And after a while, no one is even listening."

Kathleen Troia McFarland
American communications consultant

Since the kidnapping of the three teenage boys in the biblical heartland of Israel, we have been praying for their safe release and we will continue to pray. Nonetheless, we have to remember that this is an opportunity for our leaders to take real action as promised and to hold the Hamas-Fatah unity terrorist government responsible.

Now is the time not just to surround Hebron and arrest Hamas terrorists ... Now is the time to shut down Hebron and every Palestinian Authority city completely.

Shut off the electricity.

Shut off the water.

Start bombing every stronghold of Fatah, of Hamas, and of the PA. Make it clear that the bombing will not stop until the Israeli boys are handed over to the IDF.

Now is the time to enter Ramallah and take over and seal off the government complex of the PA and to confiscate their weapons, as well as the latest proof that they are paying the salaries of the terrorists.

These actions should continue at least until the boys are released.

No more compromises and enough talking. If we are truly

holding Mahmoud Abbas and his PA responsible, as Prime Minister Netanyahu and Defense Minister Yaalon proclaimed just a few days ago, it's time to take action. Real action that will serve as a deterrent that they will never forget.

Bibi, Take Off The Gloves!

"The cat with gloves catches no mice."

Navjot Singh Sidhu
Indian athlete, politician, entertainer

Whether the IDF succeeds in saving the three teenage hostages or not, we the people have a right to demand that our elected leaders stand by their words and their threats.

For weeks we have been hearing the mantra that the PA, the Palestinian Authority – AKA the Hamas AND Fatah Unity Regime – will be held accountable for any terrorist attacks. Now that it's happened, we see the IDF only going after Hamas terrorists, carefully avoiding the "innocent" civilians who voted for them, while Fatah has the honor of Netanyahu asking their assistance to find the hostages.

What he should be doing is the following:

1. Close down and destroy Mahmoud Abbas's Mukata headquarters in Ramallah, but first capture all weapons, then take and publicize all updated documents that prove that he is financing terror to this day.

2. Shut down Hebron and every PA-controlled city completely. Shut off the electricity. Shut off the water.

3. Start bombing every stronghold of Fatah, of Hamas, and of the Palestinian Authority and make it clear that the bombing will not stop until the Israeli boys are handed over safely to the IDF.

In fact, all of these actions should be continued at least until the boys are safely released. Most importantly, a clear ultimatum should be delivered to Mahmoud Abbas and all of his terrorist henchman that if the boys aren't returned alive and well within 24 hours – then every top Fatah/Hamas leader, INCLUDING ABBAS HIMSELF, will be killed.

The best defense is a good offense – and not just words.

Words, Words, Words

"Children never believe what we say, but they believe everything we do."

Elaine M. Gibson
Author, parenting advisor

Prime Minister Netanyahu has recently declared: "Abbas Will Be Judged By His Actions, Not By His Words." Is that really so? Netanyahu was referring to Abbas's public statement criticizing the kidnapping of the three Israeli teenage boys "because it hurts the Palestinian cause," while at the same time criticizing the subsequent Israeli crackdown. Obviously, it was a very two-faced and qualified condemnation, but no surprise, coming as it did, from a Holocaust denier and a slimy financier of terrorism. However, let's focus not on Abbas, but rather on the validity of the above words from our Prime Minister who, let's not forget, was put into office by us, and is responsible to us, the citizens of Israel.

Abbas's "actions" have been as follows:

1. Paying the salaries of all "Palestinian" terrorists – and he is an equal opportunity employer – he pays not just his own Fatah terrorists, but also Hamas and Islamic Jihad.

2. Naming streets and town squares in the Palestinian Authority-controlled cities after convicted Islamic terrorists, thereby honoring those who have killed and wounded thousands of Israelis.

3. Not repudiating his unity government with Hamas.

4. Brazenly violating all signed agreements with Israel.

How has Netanyahu been "judging" Abbas?

1. Calling him on the phone to ask for his help to find the teenage hostages.

2. In the IDF search for the boys, carefully only targeting Hamas and Islamic Jihad terrorists, while obviously ignoring those of Fatah – Abbas's terrorists.

3. Not "holding Abbas responsible" in any way, shape, or form – not for financing terrorism, nor for naming town squares and streets after terrorists, nor for remaining in unity with Hamas, nor for violating all signed agreements with Israel.

Perhaps it's time that we start judging our esteemed leader – Mr. Netanyahu – by HIS actions???

Obama's Deafening Silence

"Silence in the face of evil is itself evil: God will not hold us guiltless.
Not to speak is to speak. Not to act is to act."

Dietrich Bonhoeffer
German Lutheran pastor, theologian, anti-Nazi dissident

The Israeli children hostage crisis continues and most of my focus has been on the weak response of Israel's political leadership in confronting the two-headed Hamas-Fatah monster, commonly known as the Palestinian Authority (PA). While Prime Minister Netanyahu continues to tip-toe around Abbas and his Fatah terrorists, careful not to harm one hair on their heads, it's certainly not unreasonable to ask him for a public explanation of why he isn't taking a stronger approach.

After his very public threats to "hold Abbas and Fatah responsible" for the unity government with Hamas and any ensuing terrorism that emerges, what is Bibi now afraid of? Could it be that he's concerned about what the world will say, or more accurately and specifically, what President Obama will do?

And while on that topic, where is Obama? Since the three Israeli boys were kidnapped, the American president has been mysteriously silent. Yes, I know that he has his problems in Iraq, where he is now oddly supporting Iran-backed Shiite Muslims who are fighting against al-Qaeda-backed Sunni Muslims, as if either side deserves anyone's support. Nonetheless, President Obama is still ostensibly the leader of the free world (even if his career is a product of collusion between Islamic ideologues and secular Communists – he is still the President of the United States).

Historically, American presidents have been known to speak out on behalf of freedom. Therefore, wouldn't it be correct for Israel to expect a few strong words of moral support and perhaps even an American demand that the Hamas-Fatah PA immediately free the three teenagers?

The obvious problem is that Obama, Kerry, and yes Hillary Clinton, as well, are so heavily invested in the Hamas-Fatah PA and are so anti-Jewish "settler" that they have lost any semblance of humanity. To them, any Jew who lives in his ancestral homeland and dares to set foot in the biblical heartland of Judea or Samaria is an "obstacle to peace," and therefore, somehow deserves to be attacked, or in this case, kidnapped. The sad reality is that Barack Hussein Obama and his cronies are no friends of Israel, and never have been, but we are talking here about the kidnapping of Israeli children, and the inhumane silence from the White House has been heard in Israel – loud and clear.

In any event, we can only rely on the Almighty, and He will stand with us if we act strongly in the spirit of Joshua and King David to obliterate our enemies – and the Hamas-Fatah Palestinian Authority is indeed a bitter enemy. Sadly, much of the world will continue to condemn us, but we will continue to grow, to build, and to defend our nation.

As Israel's first Prime Minister David Ben-Gurion once said, "What matters is not what the goyim (the nations) say, but what the Jews do."

Peres and Abbas (And Arafat): Partners Indeed

"A solution of two national states – a Jewish state, Israel; an Arab state, Palestine. The Palestinians are our closest neighbors. I believe they may become our closest friends."

Shimon Peres
Former Israeli President

"On the anniversary of the (Fatah) Launch, we renew the promise to our blessed Martyrs, that we will follow the path of the Martyr Brother Yasser Arafat and his comrades among the leaders of all the fighting forces, all the Martyrs."

Mahmoud Abbas
Palestinian Authority President

Outgoing Israeli President Shimon Peres continues to heap voluminous words of praise on Palestinian Authority (PA) President Mahmoud Abbas, describing him as "the best partner that Israel has and the best we have had. I've known him for twenty years and he's a man of his word and of courage ... We shouldn't miss an opportunity to make peace with him."

Despite criticizing the kidnapping, Abbas, who, unlike his Hamas colleagues knows well how to speak out of both sides of his mouth, has recently accused Israel of "killing Palestinians in cold blood," and has denied that there is "credible information" that his PA unity partner Hamas is responsible for the kidnapping. Furthermore, Abbas's PA is the world's largest employer of terrorists and brazenly continues to pay the salaries of the Fatah, Hamas, and Islamic Jihad terrorists to this very day, having continued and institutionalized the vile system that was originally put in place by his notorious predecessor, Yasser Arafat.

Peres, who has lived for over 90 years, is smart enough to know that by calling Abbas a partner, he is essentially praising and justifying this partner's clearly documented financing of terrorism against Israeli citizens. Given Mr. Peres's shameful record as the architect of the Oslo Accords, which caused the greatest waves of terrorism in Israel's history, his recurring, flowery praise of Abbas should come as no surprise.

Abbas is indeed an appropriate partner for Peres, for the two have enabled the bus bombings, the ambushes, and yes, the kidnappings. Many thousands of us, Israelis who were wounded and maimed by "Palestinian" bullets, rocks, and bombs, yet survived, will not forget the self-serving arrogance of this false peace promoter. We will not forgive, not because we oppose forgiveness, but because we cannot forgive those who don't sincerely request forgiveness. Peres has never shown any remorse for his actions that have torn apart and traumatized so many Israeli families and communities. And we certainly won't forget his crimes, for to do so would be a betrayal of the many thousands of Jews who were brutally killed or wounded, all for the glory of his beloved "peace process." And that is sadly, as he leaves office, the true legacy of Shimon Peres.

Feel-Good Gatherings
Will Not Defeat Terrorist Enemies

Life is a song – sing it.
Life is a game – play it.
Life is a challenge – meet it.

Sai Baba
Indian guru and spiritual leader

A large gathering of Jews uniting to show concern about the hostages is good, but not good enough. It's time to have a more serious mass protest and to shout, "I'm mad as hell and I'm not gonna take it anymore!" Maybe then the politicians will stop talking about what they are doing, and will start listening to those who are calling for more offensive action.

With all due respect to the sing-along gathering this evening in Tel Aviv calling for the release of the three teenage hostages, it should be clear by now that Hamas doesn't feel at all threatened by Jews singing in unison, and that there are much more effective ways to bring the boys home. Yes, any mass gathering that encourages unity is positive and unity may have spiritual ramifications that can influence the situation in a good way, but it's much more important to demand of the politicians who we elected to office to take serious action against the terrorists and the thousands of civilians who support them. The followings steps by our political leadership are needed:

1.   Stop babbling about the "heavy price" to be paid

for terrorism against Israelis and about "the long arm" that will reach the terrorists. Neither Hamas, nor Fatah, nor Islamic Jihad are impressed by mere words.

2. Continue searching for the boys, continue intelligence gathering, and continue rounding up the terrorists, but promise to the public – and quickly put it into law – that you will stop releasing terrorists – and it doesn't matter if there is intense pressure from the Obama administration or from the media, as in the horrible Gilad Shalit deal. No more terrorist prisoner releases, period.

3. Start hitting their civilians and yes, disrupting their daily lives, by shutting off their electricity, which they don't pay for anyhow, and shutting off their water. Then demand information leading to the release of the hostages, if they want to return to their daily routines.

4. If that doesn't convince them, start massive bombing of targets in Hebron, Shechem, Gaza, and every other Arab-occupied city in Judea and Samaria, and continue to raise the volume until they release the hostages safely to their families.

5. Confiscate all bombs, guns, and other weapons from Hamas, Fatah, Islamic Jihad, and all other terrorists in the PA cities and towns and in all of the liberated areas under Israel's control – in other words – areas A, B, and C in Judea and Samaria – the so-called West Bank. Those weapons will otherwise be used to kidnap other Israeli children.

Songs are nice, prayer is good, and unity has value, but

until we truly turn on the military faucet full-force against our enemies, this will continue to be a recurring nightmare for all of us. Remember Dresden, remember Berlin, remember Nagasaki, and remember Hiroshima. In all of those places, the Americans and/or their allies massively bombed cities – killing many enemy civilians and causing the enemy to surrender. The only way to win is by hitting them very, very hard and ignoring international condemnation. There is no need to feel guilty about killing civilians who voted at least 95% for Hamas and for Fatah – two of the world's most notorious terrorist organizations.

Singing and crying together is understandable and positive, but it's time to demand real action.

Destroy The Enemy:
Time For The Gaza First Plan

"The enemies you make by taking a decided stand generally have more respect for you than the friends you make by being on the fence."

Henry Kissinger
Former US Secretary of State

For eighteen days, I have been calling for strong offensive action against the terrorists of the Palestinian Authority – both Hamas and Fatah – as the best way to find the teenage hostages and to deter future kidnappings and other terrorist attacks. Now that the boys have been found dead, the justification and necessity for very strong offensive action is even greater.

It should come as no shock that the boys were murdered, for this is the mentality of the Islamic terrorist that is sworn to the destruction of Israel and doesn't distinguish between soldiers and civilians.

We Jews are different. We respect life. However, in a time of war, the rules are not the same, and we are certainly in an ongoing war for our survival. Saul, the first king of ancient Israel, was removed from the throne by Samuel the Prophet because he didn't completely obliterate the enemy's animals, even though he did destroy virtually all of the enemy's people.

Yes, Saul was in defiance of a specific command to obliterate the Amalekites, but the general lesson for our times is clear: When fighting a war against an enemy, the enemy must be destroyed, and decisively, without excessive concern for who is an active soldier.

However, the first step is to identify the enemy. In this case, the enemy is not just Hamas, which kidnapped and murdered the teenage boys and has been firing rockets at Israeli cities from their strongholds in Gaza for years. The enemy is also Fatah, which in addition to its own horrific list of terrorist attacks, sits proudly in a unity coalition with Hamas and pays the substantial salaries of all of the terrorists.

And yes, the enemy is also the civilians who voted these two terrorist organizations into power. Not every German was an active Nazi, just as not every Gazan is an active Hamas member, and not every Arab resident of Samaria is an active member of Fatah paying the terrorists to kill Jewish children.

Nonetheless, an enemy is an enemy and the only way to win this war is to destroy the enemy, without excessive regard for who is a soldier and who is a civilian. In Dresden, in Berlin, in Nagasaki, and in Hiroshima, the Americans and/or their allies massively bombed enemy-controlled cities into submission, killing hundreds of thousands of enemy civilians and causing the enemy's political leadership to surrender. The only way to win a war is by hitting them very, very hard and ignoring international condemnation.

Last but not least, we Jews will always aim our bombs primarily at military targets, but there is absolutely no need to feel guilty about "disrupting the lives of," and killing or wounding enemy civilians who are almost entirely Hamas and Fatah supporters. Yes, it is absolutely relevant to point out that they are staunch supporters of two of the world's most notorious terrorist organizations that are sworn to Israel's destruction, and therefore, they are our enemy.

It's time for the new Gaza First Plan – Let the bombing rounds begin on the Hamas-controlled cities of Gaza and may the bombing soon extend to the Mukata – PA/Fatah

President Mahmoud Abbas's PA terrorist headquarters in Ramallah, which should be totally leveled to the ground. Yes, destroy the Hamas in Gaza completely, until the white flags of surrender will decorate the streets, but then focus on totally disarming and dismantling the Fatah-dominated Palestinian Authority that has been paying the salaries of all the terrorists for many years, including those of the Hamas.

Destroy the enemy. The time to act and to act decisively is now.

The Murders And Zionism: Time For Answers

"Thou shalt not murder."

Exodus 20:13

The brutal murders of the three kidnapped boys have revealed terrible flaws in the system of terrorism prevention, but it's not just technical errors that need correction. The flawed police response to Gilad Sha'ar's emergency call that was ignored is but a symptom of a dysfunctional Zionism that has forgotten its purpose.

Prime Minister Binyamin Netanyahu and his Defense Minister Moshe Yaalon have spent the past eighteen months making vacuous pronouncements about how Israel will hit the Hamas terrorists with "heavy punishment" and that "the long arm of Israel" will reach them. Other politicians in the coalition have warned of a "proper Zionist response," independent of military action. Indeed, it behooves us to examine just what that proper Zionist response should be.

I hereby call on the leaders of Israel to:

1. End the shameful, unofficial freeze in the granting of building permits to Jews in Judea and Samaria, in eastern Jerusalem, and in all parts of the liberated land of Israel. Every resident of Judea and Samaria knows that the supply of housing is much less than the demand. This is due to an unofficial Netanyahu-Yaalon policy of choking the Jewish residents of Judea and Samaria by stifling their natural growth.

2. Establish a new Jewish city in the heart of Samaria. It is an outright betrayal of Zionism that the current government is aiding and abetting (in cooperation with the Americans) the building of Rawabi, a new Arab city in the heart of Samaria, while consistently preventing the establishment of any new Jewish communities.

3. Adopt the Levy Report as official government policy, which will immediately give the legal backing for a proud Jewish settlement policy.

4. Pass the Knesset bill affirming Israel as the nation-state of the Jewish People.

5. Require Zionist-Jewish education in every school in Israel. The amazing Jewish return to the Land of Israel in our times is a prophetic process that all segments of the population need to learn about.

Apologies to a world that hates us won't work, nor will pompous meaningless statements that aren't followed by action. The five points listed above are the minimal steps that are needed to restore Zionism to its Jewish roots. Are Netanyahu and Yaalon prepared to meet the challenge?

Enemy Civilians – And Ours

"Hamas, they are using civilians' lives, they are using children, they are using the suffering of people every day to achieve their goals. And this is what I hate."

Mosab Hassan Yousef
Son of one of the Hamas founders, Sheikh Hassan Yousef

After the posting of my article, "Destroy The Enemy: Time For The Gaza First Plan," I received a large volume of comments and feedback, mostly very positive, but as is often the case when a sensitive nerve is struck, I received a few responses complaining about my willingness to harm the non-combat enemy in Gaza, otherwise known as civilians. Here is my response to one such letter:

Dear Yaakov,
Concerning your letter in which you said "I just read a comment on FB (Facebook) and they posted an article that u wrote *advocating killing all the Palestinians*" (emphasis mine).
People may interpret as they wish, and that often stems from their own biases, but I suggest that you read my words more carefully. The above words are a misquote.
What I wrote is as follows:
It should come as no shock that the boys were murdered, for this is the mentality of the Islamic terrorist that is sworn to the destruction of Israel and doesn't distinguish between soldiers and civilians.
We Jews are different. We respect life. However, in a time

of war, the rules are not the same, and we are certainly in an ongoing war for our survival.

Nonetheless, an enemy is an enemy and the only way to win this war is to destroy the enemy, without excessive regard for who is a soldier and who is a civilian. In Dresden, in Berlin, in Nagasaki, and in Hiroshima, the Americans and/or their allies massively bombed enemy-controlled cities into submission, killing hundreds of thousands of enemy civilians and causing the enemy's political leadership to surrender.

Last but not least, we Jews will always aim our bombs primarily at military targets, but there is absolutely no need to feel guilty about "disrupting the lives of," and killing or wounding enemy civilians who are almost entirely Hamas and Fatah supporters. Yes, it is absolutely relevant to point out that they are staunch supporters of two of the world's most notorious terrorist organizations that are sworn to Israel's destruction, and therefore, they are our enemy.

As the Allies did in WWII, and as I wrote in the article, the rules of wartime are different, and indeed, we are in a state of war. I, for one, am not prepared to put our civilians' nor our soldiers' lives in danger in order to protect the enemy civilians.

Bibi, Take Back The Weapons!

"Let me make a short, opening, blanket comment. There are no good guns. There are no bad guns. Any gun in the hands of a bad man is a bad thing. Any gun in the hands of a decent person is no threat to anybody – except bad people ..."

Charlton Heston
American actor, NBC's Meet the Press, 1997

When I visited Israel for the first time in 1983, the so-called Palestinians had hardly any weapons and were not a serious threat to Israel. As the implementation of the Oslo Accords progressed in the early 1990s, Israel foolishly gave substantial amounts of weapons to the newly-formed Palestinian Authority, our new "partner for peace." The stated purpose was to provide their "police" (Fatah) with the means to contain "the terrorists" (Hamas).

It always went unspoken among the Israeli officials who enabled the transfer of these weapons that the Fatah and its "military wings," such as the al-Aqsa Martyrs Brigades and the Tanzim militia, who committed countless horrific terrorist attacks against Israelis, were the ultimate recipients of this unexpected military largess, which has multiplied exponentially ever since we first opened the floodgates.

With the exception of occasional raids and a few mini-wars, Israel's political leadership has allowed the Palestinian Authority and its Hamas-Fatah terrorist components to keep and increase their weapons supply, which they continue to use against us.

Therefore, it needs to be stated and stated clearly for every Israeli to hear: Israel's leadership – from Yitzhak Rabin to Binyamin Netanyahu – bears ultimate responsibility for virtually every terrorist attack that has taken place since the signing of the Oslo Accords and every subsequent agreement.

Having said that, we need to learn the lessons from those tragic mistakes. Simply put, it's time to take back those weapons. In the eighteen days that all of Israel was obsessed with the kidnapping of our three teenagers, the IDF was given a free hand to search and capture weapons in the PA-autonomous areas. This process needs to continue and be greatly expanded as a full-blown ongoing weapons collection until we return the situation to what existed back in 1983. It is an absolute danger and a betrayal of Israel's citizens to allow any of these weapons to remain in their hands.

Would such an ongoing operation in Gaza, Judea, and Samaria arouse international opposition? Of course it would. The primary responsibility of Israel's leaders is to protect its citizens, not to adhere to the diktats of foreign leaders.

Be courageous, act strongly, and fear not the condemnations from the UN, the EU, and the US State Department. Take back the weapons!

A Nation Of Moldy Doormats?

"If you act like a doormat, people will walk all over you."

Unknown

T he repeated calls for Israeli restraint in responding to rocket attacks emanating from Gaza would be comical, if it wasn't so bizarre. What other nation would accept rocket attacks on its cities, while just retaliating with tit for tat counter-attacks?

The unjust criticism from the Obama administration, from the EU, and from the UN demand a response, but not just in words. We are not a nation of moldy doormats and we have the right not just to respond to such rocket attacks, but to create a strong deterrence to such attacks. That will only happen when we realize that tit for tat retaliation doesn't work.

What I propose is very simple – multiples of ten. For every 5 rocket attacks from Gaza, we respond with 50. For every 50, we respond with 500. They will get the message loud and clear. If the attacks continue, increase the multiples until they beg for mercy. That is how wars are won, and we are indeed in a war with a bitter enemy.

And how do we respond to unjustified world criticism? Explain and Ignore. No proud nation in its right mind allows other nations and biased world bodies to force it to undermine its national security. The criticism will only begin to die down when we act like a nation with national pride and responsibility for the security of its citizens. Yes, we should explain and we should explain well, but if the critics persist in their biases, we need to learn to ignore the haters of Israel and to act in our national interest.

The other nations will only respect a nation that respects itself.

Responding To Criticism:
Explain And Ignore!

"If you can't explain it simply, you don't understand it well enough."

Albert Einstein, Nobel Laureate

My last blog post has just become very relevant as Israel has begun to take a more offensive approach in hitting back against the rocket attacks from Gaza, and therefore, those words need to be repeated, albeit in revised format.

Now that PA Chairman Mahmoud Abbas is threatening to go to the international community demanding that Israel stop its air counter-strikes on Gaza, we can already anticipate that the unwieldy family of nations will soon join the chorus of harsh criticism against Israel for responding to rocket attacks on its major cities. As Israel fights back more and more, the cynical calls for "Israeli restraint" will continue to grow.

We have been in this movie before and it isn't a good one. The repeated calls for Israeli restraint in responding to rocket attacks emanating from Gaza would be comical, if they weren't so bizarre. What other nation would accept rocket attacks on its cities, while just retaliating with tit for tat counter-attacks?

Such criticism demands a bold response, but not just in words. Israel is not a nation of moldy doormats and we have the right not just to respond to such rocket attacks, but to create a strong deterrence to such attacks. That will only happen when we realize that tit for tat retaliation doesn't work.

What I have proposed is very simple – multiples of ten. For every 5 rocket attacks from Gaza, we respond with 50. For every 50, we respond with 500. They will get the message loud and clear. If the attacks continue, increase the multiples until they beg for mercy. That is how wars are won, and we are indeed in a war with a bitter enemy.

And how do we respond to unjustified world criticism? Explain and Ignore. No proud nation in its right mind allows other nations and biased world bodies to force it to undermine its national security. The criticism will only begin to die down when we act like a nation with national pride and responsibility for the security of its citizens. Yes, we should explain and we should explain well, but if the critics persist in their biases, we need to learn to ignore the haters of Israel and to act in our national interest.

The other nations will only respect a nation that respects itself.

This Time Fight To Win

"But I will send a fire on the wall of Gaza ..."

Amos 1:7

Dateline November 2012: It was a humiliating spectacle. All of Israel, not to mention the thousands of reservist soldiers amassed along the Gazan border, was waiting anxiously for the IDF ground offensive that would stop the Hamas rocket fire once and for all, but an unexpected press conference was held at which Prime Minister Binyamin Netanyahu and Foreign Minister Avigdor Liberman announced their acceptance of an Egyptian-brokered ceasefire arrangement before the ground operation had even begun. Meanwhile, the streets of Gaza were filled with the haters of Israel celebrating the Israeli retreat with "victory candy" being handed out in the streets.

Just two years later, there are hundreds of rockets being fired daily, now with a range that is reaching all major Israeli cities. With tensions again rising along the Gazan border in anticipation of an impending Israeli ground offensive, and with tens of thousands of our reservists being called up, the question must once again be asked of our political leadership: Will the job be done properly this time?

By now it should be clear to all that no Israeli offensive will be successful unless:

1.   All arms-smuggling tunnels are completely destroyed.

2.   Israel retakes the strategic Philadelphi Corridor, along the border with Egypt.

3.   All bomb factories and warehouses are totally destroyed.

4.   All Hamas, Islamic Jihad, and Fatah weapons in Gaza are confiscated.

While those are the minimal requirements for any Israeli offensive to be considered a victory, there are other goals that would certainly be advisable, such as:

1.   Totally eliminate the Palestinian Authority as a political force that Israel foolishly accepts as a "peace partner."

2.   Confiscate all weapons in Judea and Samaria and Jerusalem – that includes Islamic Jihad, Hamas and its unity government partner Fatah, as well.

3.   Take full control of Gaza and reestablish the formerly thriving Jewish communities in place of the rocket launchers now occupying that sacred ground.

4.   Launch a major public relations offensive, unapologetically explaining our justification for this offensive, followed by Israeli resolve to ignore those who refuse to accept our absolutely legitimate explanations.

Last but not least, we must all be united in prayer for the success of this operation. If we are strong and courageous and allow our soldiers to fight in the spirit of Joshua, the battle will be won. If not, the candy will again be distributed in the streets of Gaza as the missiles fall on Tel Aviv and Jerusalem.

Ceasefire Madness – Again

"No compromise with the main purpose, no peace till victory, no pact with unrepentant wrong."

Winston Churchill, British Statesman

Once again, we are being confronted with the humiliating spectacle of an Israeli political leadership pleading for defeat rather than victory, as the Egyptian ceasefire proposal is currently being considered by the Israeli Cabinet.

Once again, the thousands of ground troops, trained to defeat the enemy, may be left stranded on the Gazan border without having completed the job that had been started by the air and naval forces.

Once again, the words of Prime Minister Binyamin (Bibi) Netanyahu and Defense Minister Moshe (Bogie) Yaalon will have been proven to be meaningless threats from frightened men with no spiritual backbones.

Once again, the fear of the nations and the lack of belief in the righteousness of our fight for the Land of Israel will have caused a failed military operation.

Perhaps it will be different from what it seems now as these words are being written, and perhaps the Cabinet will reject the ceasefire proposal, but the very fact that it is being brought to a vote in the Cabinet shows that Bibi and Bogie are already beginning to cave in. Such a lack of determination will defeat the aims of the operation, will hurt Israel's deterrence, will encourage the terrorists, and will betray Israel's citizens. And if that happens, it will be very, very sad.

Bibi and Bogie:
The Land Is Acquired Through Sacrifice

"Three things are acquired through suffering: Torah, the Land of Israel and the World to Come."

The Talmud

B ibi and Bogie are wrong again.
Prime Minister Netanyahu (Bibi) and Defense Minister Yaalon (Bogie) have mistakenly delivered the message that the Egyptian-brokered and US-pressured ceasefire will bring long-term quiet to our volatile region and that we should avoid what could be a messy ground war. Bibi has reinforced that message by firing his Deputy Defense Minister Danny Danon for criticizing the proposed ceasefire, even though virtually everyone here in Israel knows that the war will not be won decisively without sending in the ground troops.

Most of the Cabinet voted for the ceasefire, but guess what? In a show of Islamic pride, the ceasefire has been rejected by Hamas, which is now making new demands in exchange for their adherence to any negotiated agreement. They seem to have the fortitude and determination that we should ironically be able to learn from, even though they have learned that very determination from the founding fathers and mothers of Zionism.

The Hamas terrorists apparently have learned well our Talmudic maxim – "Three things are acquired through great suffering – Torah, the Land of Israel, and the World to Come." The tragedy is that they seem to understand it better than Israel's current political leadership.

The great Torah sage, the Vilna Gaon, teaches us that one who is willing to sacrifice for the Land of Israel will acquire it completely.

Nobody in Israel wants to see our soldiers killed or wounded, but the nation that is willing to suffer and to sacrifice for its land will win the war.

Hillary Clinton
On Israel And Palestine

"He who sacrifices a whole offering shall be rewarded for a whole offering; he who offers a burnt-offering shall have the reward of a burnt-offering; but he who offers humility to God and man shall be rewarded with a reward as if he had offered all the sacrifices in the world."

The Talmud

I've just read an A7 (israelnationalnews.com) news item entitled, "Hillary Sides with Israel vs. Jon Stewart" and watched the entire video of the actual interview. While it's true that she didn't go for blaming Israel for a "humanitarian crisis" in Gaza, she didn't exactly "side" with Israel, although I wish that she had.

What I heard in that extensive interview are the same old tired beliefs that the "land for peace" formula can work, which would mean that Israel has to surrender most of its biblical heartland to several armed bands of Islamic terrorists. We see what such a formula has brought us in Gaza. It doesn't matter whether we call it The Road to Peace or The Two State Solution, this approach has always failed and will continue to fail because it raises unrealistic and very unjustified expectations on the part of the Arabs by ignoring some basic facts:

1.   The historic Land of Israel (even if you use the old Roman-coined name, Palestina or Palestine) is the God-given inheritance of the Jewish people.

2.   The Land of Israel was the sovereign homeland of the nation of Israel until we were exiled from the land, with the height of our full sovereignty reached during the kingdoms of King David and King Solomon.

3.   Most of the Arabs currently living in the Land of Israel moved here after the Jews started returning home in large numbers in the early 20th century and creating an economy in the Land of Israel, thus providing work that attracted Arabs from throughout the region.

4.   There was never an Arab nor a Muslim country called Palestine in the Land of Israel, nor anywhere for that matter.

If Hillary doubts #4, she should answer the following questions:

1.   What was the national anthem of that country called Palestine?

2.   Who was the first elected or non-elected leader of that country?

3.   What was the monetary currency of that country?

Undoubtedly, this woman who aspires to be the next president of the United States can't answer the above questions, because there never was such a country. If she and her colleagues like Obama, Kerry, and husband Bill would admit that there is no historical justification for creating such a nation-state, on what basis would they create it? Would it be on the basis of the "Palestinian people's" autonomous areas having the most terrorists per square meter or would it be based on their creating a terrorist unity government?

Or perhaps it would be on the basis of the "Palestinian people" having the dubious honor of intentionally killing and wounding the most Jewish civilians since the Holocaust?

I would humbly suggest that Ms. Clinton do some reading before aiming to become the American commander-in-chief and leader of the free world. I'd be happy to offer my services in furthering that sorely needed educational process.

No More Hesitation

"And having thus chosen our course, without guile, and with pure purpose, let us renew our trust in God, and go forward without fear, and with manly hearts."

Abraham Lincoln
American President, 1861

Israeli ground troops have just entered Gaza en masse with the stated objective to destroy Hamas's hundreds of weapons and terrorist smuggling tunnels.

As I have been urging Israel's leaders in my previous articles, this time Israel needs to forcefully fight to win.

By now it is becoming clear to a growing majority in Israel that no Israeli offensive will be successful unless:

1.   All arms-smuggling tunnels are completely destroyed.

2.   Israel retakes the strategic Philadelphi Corridor, along the border with Egypt.

3.   All bomb factories and warehouses are totally destroyed.

4.   All Hamas, Islamic Jihad, and Fatah weapons are confiscated.

These are the minimal steps needed to stop the rocket fire and to end the Gaza-based terrorists' ability to create havoc in our lives.

Wishing our soldiers great success and urging Israel's political leadership to follow through to victory!

Restraint Is Not A Virtue

"The battle, sir, is not to the strong alone; it is to the vigilant, the active, the brave."

Patrick Henry
Central figure in the American revolution

"Those who are kind to the cruel, will ultimately be cruel to those who are kind."

Midrash Yalkut Shimoni

Restraint that imperils the lives of Israel's citizens is a patently un-Jewish concept.
It is indeed the epitome of chutzpah – and an absolute injustice – for President Obama, the EU, the UN, and others to demand that Israel employ restraint in a war that was launched by the Hamas terrorists, even if they are partners in the "respectable" Palestinian Authority. Israel had been exceptional in its restraint from retaliation for years, foolishly looking the other way, while Hamas built hundreds of tunnels to smuggle in weapons and to infiltrate Israel with its terrorists. All of this with barely a peep from the free world.

Israel never targets civilians, but when terrorists use schools, hospitals, and private homes as human shields, which is indeed a war crime, it is nothing short of immoral for anyone to complain when enemy civilians get killed.

Having said all that, let's not forget – These are the same civilians who overwhelmingly elected the Jew-hating Hamas terrorist organization to head their government. Why should

Israel shed any tears when those who are killed or wounded, are those who are knowingly shielding Hamas or Islamic Jihad terrorists and their weapons or bomb factories?

Every general in the free world knows that you cannot win a war – and a very justified war at that – by shooting rubber bullets or by giving the enemy 48 hours advance warning to evacuate a bomb factory. Israel should ignore the sanctimonious shrieks of the deceptive Jihadist spin doctors, as well as those of the self-righteous leftists who have never experienced the pain of Islamic terrorism.

Restraint is not a virtue in and of itself. It's time to bring the fight to Israel's enemy and to do so with heads held high, for this is indeed a righteous war.

Warning The Enemy Kills Our Soldiers

"Israel is the only nation in history of the world that has found a way to mass-produce dumb Jews."

Sidney Zion, Author

Is the Israeli army moral or suicidal? For several years, our political and military leaders have been proudly reciting the national mantra – about the extensive warnings that we give before we attack an enemy. This proclamation is repeated over and over to the world media during our many wars, all to counter the unfair charge that we are excessively harming civilians.

It is now being reported that thirteen Israeli soldiers are dead in the terrorist stronghold of Shejaiya in Gaza, after advance warning was given by the IDF to leave the area because the IDF would be attacking soon. Hamas was well prepared, apparently using the advance notification to plant explosives and to prepare ambushes well ahead of time, thereby putting our soldiers at a disadvantage.

Nobody wants to say the truth, because we know that our political leadership is under heavy pressure from Obama, Kerry, the EU, and the UN, who claim to be concerned about civilian casualties. None of us want to be seen as undermining our prime minister with criticism that will make it difficult for him, but it needs to be said and stated clearly:

The warnings given in advance of attacks – the leaflets dropped from the sky, the text messages, and so on are putting our soldiers in danger. Not only the Gaza Arab civilians get the warning messages, but also the Hamas and Islamic

Jihad terrorists, and especially their leadership that has been planning for years for this scenario. They exploit our political defensiveness to defeat us militarily by eliminating our deterrence. It's a sophisticated, yet simple game of psychological warfare and they are winning.

Every general in the free world knows that you cannot win a war – even a very justified war like this one – by essentially giving the enemy 48 hours advance warning to evacuate a bomb factory or to plant booby traps with which to ambush our soldiers. Israel should ignore the private lectures of self-righteous, yet disingenuous politicians like John Kerry, recently caught off camera blasting Israel for harming civilians, yet publicly spouting empty words referring to our right of self-defense.

The IDF is not an organization of public relations apologists and should only be in the business of winning wars by defeating the enemy – speedily, decisively, and completely. For our political leadership to continue this risky political game of national suicide through pathetic apologetics is a danger to our soldiers and to their ability to win.

Just Say No

"May God defend me from my friends: I can defend myself from my enemies."

Voltaire
French philosopher, playwright

US President Barack Obama and his Secretary of State John Kerry share a peculiar habit of speaking out of both sides of their mouths. Since the beginning of Operation Protective Edge in Gaza, both of these men have been proclaiming Israel's "right to self-defense," while at the same time calling for an "immediate ceasefire."

Guess what? It is a contradiction in terms. Israel is finally fighting back after five consecutive years of virtually no retaliation to Hamas, Islamic Jihad, and yes, Fatah aggression against Israel. For five long years, Israel's political leadership has been pressured by the sanctimonious, pompous president in DC to restrain itself, to only occasionally hit back, and even then, with at least one arm tied behind its back.

Mr. Kerry, who was unintentionally caught on camera yesterday sarcastically complaining about Israel harming civilians in Gaza, is on his way to the Middle East on a mission. And what is the goal of his mission? Kerry wants to achieve an immediate ceasefire that would put an immediate halt to Israel's painstaking efforts to destroy the weapons/terrorist smuggling tunnels, the bomb factories, the missile-launching pads, and the weapons warehouses.

With "friends" like these defending our right to self-defense, we would do well to remember former First Lady Nancy Reagan's slogan, albeit in her war on illicit drug use by American youth:

"Just Say No" would be a very appropriate slogan for Israel's leaders to adopt as they await Kerry's arrival. Any other response would be an insult to our soldiers, who are valiantly fighting in Gaza for the safety of all of Israel. Yes, give him the respect that a world leader deserves. Explain clearly why we need to continue and broaden the operation. Explain why most Israelis are standing together in support of the war effort. Then ignore what will most likely be his unjust demands for an immediate ceasefire, which if implemented, would bring back the rocket attacks in full force within two years, and possibly much sooner.

Just Say No.

Airlines Halt Flights:
Should We Blame the Messenger?

"Don't blame the messenger because the message is unpleasant."

Ken Starr,
American lawyer, prosecutor

The blame game over the sudden halt of foreign flights to Israel is certainly one of the more interesting chapters in the ongoing Gaza story. There are those who are blaming the Americans for using the rocket attack on the town of Yehud near Ben Gurion International Airport as a pretext to pressure Israel to agree to a ceasefire. Indeed, US Secretary of State John Kerry's arrival in Israel with that stated purpose in mind seems to give credence to the charge of an inappropriate use of economic pressure to achieve a political goal.

Having said all that, those of us who believe that the Obama administration has generally been economically supportive, but politically hostile to Israel, should avoid the blame-game on this issue. The sad truth is that for five years, Israel's political leadership irresponsibly ignored the hornet's nest that is called Gaza, hoping that peace negotiations with Fatah – our supposed partners in peace – would somehow be successful and that meanwhile, the rockets wouldn't cause us any serious damage. Well, it didn't work. The Hamas and Islamic Jihad terrorists, and even some from Fatah, continued to build up their rocket launching capabilities, until we have arrived at the present state of affairs, in which the rockets can reach the greater Tel Aviv area, including the airport.

Should we be surprised that the American aviators and others are genuinely nervous about the safety of their passengers? After the recent downing of the Malaysian plane over the Ukraine, such concerns are not unwarranted. However, to blame the White House is an inappropriate use of the Freudian defense mechanism called "projection," in which we ascribe our faults to others. The fact is, that Israel's political leadership cannot avoid responsibility for allowing the security situation to get to this point. Now that doesn't mean that the folks in Washington are not culpable in any way. Obama, Clinton, and Kerry have spent much of the last five years pressuring Israel not to retaliate against its enemies – not Hamas, not Islamic Jihad, not Hezbollah, and not Iran.

The potential harm to the economy of such a halt to air travel can't be ignored, but all is not lost. By making war – and this time fighting to win – against Hamas and Islamic Jihad in Gaza, we have the potential to finally put an end to the rocket attacks that are threatening Israel's economy, as well as directly hurting its citizens.

It behooves our political leadership to go forward with a broad and bold vision to the future. Our international relations can be greatly improved, not by giving in to foreign pressure, but by standing firm in defense of our national security interests, in defense of our economy, and in defense of our citizens. Those interests will be served by giving the IDF a green light to continue its valiant efforts in defense of the homeland.

America's Gift
To Hamas And Islamic Jihad

"A doubtful friend is worse than a certain enemy. Let a man be one thing or the other, and we then know how to meet him."

Aesop, Aesop's Fables

B arack Obama and John Kerry, in another strange public show of disdain for Israel, have announced a $47 million gift to the Hamas and Islamic Jihad terrorist organizations in Gaza. France quickly followed suit. Not wanting to miss a chance to show their anti-Israel bonafides, France rushed to promise an additional $14.8 million.

Yes, I know, the aid has been couched in the guise of "humanitarian aid," but is there really any doubt about who is in charge in Gaza? Does any honest person trust the Islamic terrorist organizations to distribute band-aids and bottled water to the children of Gaza? As any Hamas terrorist will tell you in a candid moment, the money will serve the urgent humanitarian need of repairing the damage that those "disproportionate Israelis" have done to the weapons and terrorist-smuggling tunnels. But that's not all. The funds will also be used for the noble humanitarian purpose of fixing the rocket-launching pads that have been impaired during the conflict.

History has shown that Hamas, not to mention its more "moderate" Fatah partner in the Palestinian Authority, has always used humanitarian aid for its evil military purpose – to kill as many Israeli children as possible and to psychologically traumatize as many Israeli children as possible. As opposed to Israel that gives top priority to civilian needs in a time of war, such as bomb shelters and civil defense, the Islamic terrorists have always exploited foreign aid to build rockets and tunnels and military summer camps for young children. While our children learn how to swim, theirs learn to use AK-47 assault rifles and to give the Nazi salute.

Obama and Kerry, as the leaders of the free world, have inadvertently exposed their true colors by standing with the enemies of Israel in these difficult days. Friends of Israel don't give millions in support to the enemy of an American ally in a time of war.

War Criminals At The UN

"You must clean your courtyards and do not follow in the footsteps of the Jews."

United Nations Relief and Works Agency's website,
Quoting from the Islamic Hadith in a post asking for support
(Quickly removed after criticism)

Here we go again. The United Nations Relief and Works Agency (UNRWA) is charging that Israel didn't allow civilians to leave one of its schools in Gaza before attacking the Islamic terrorists that were based inside and were shooting at Israeli soldiers. The Israeli government announced that it would investigate this latest incident, then cried foul, claiming that the charges are untrue.

For how long will we Israelis allow ourselves to be defensive pawns in this cynical game of having to "investigate" every time these ridiculous charges are made? For years, Hamas and Islamic Jihad terrorists have been using UNRWA schools as military bases. If UNRWA had any true sense of ethics or moral conscience, it would have closed down these "schools" a long time ago and charged Hamas and Islamic Jihad with war crimes for invading their schools and holding children and UNRWA staff as hostages.

Time for a reality check. Could it possibly be that the injustice-seekers at UNRWA are actually accomplices in these war crimes? By allowing the Hamas and Islamic Jihad terrorists to use UNRWA schools as military bases, without a word of protest in the UN Security Council or in the world media, the self-righteous crybabies at UNRWA are exposing themselves as actual accomplices in the use of children as human shields.

And that is a war crime.

No To Ceasefires – Yes To Victory

"We will have no truce or parlay with you (Hitler), or the grisly gang who work your wicked will. You do your worst – and we will do our best."

Winston Churchill, British Statesman

As Israel continues to agree to more unilateral "humanitarian" ceasefires, another soldier has been killed in Gaza. Israel continues to lose the momentum each time a ceasefire is agreed to, while Hamas and Islamic Jihad receive a much-needed respite to reorganize, to prepare new booby traps for Israeli soldiers in the alleyways of Gaza and to kill more Israeli soldiers, while we hope that maybe a few folks overseas will praise our "restraint."

Yes, there have been many successes so far and the IDF is certainly fighting a noble and difficult battle, but the surreal "operation" that we are afraid to call a war continues to stop and start, stop and start, all in order to please Barack Obama and John Kerry and to show the world that we are really nice, that we really want peace, that we really want to preserve "dignity" for all of the inhabitants of Gaza.

Aren't these the same inhabitants of Gaza who overwhelmingly voted Hamas into power? Aren't these the same inhabitants of Gaza who encourage their children and themselves to be used as human shields to prevent attacks by the IDF? And what about the "moderate wing" of the Palestinian Authority – The Fatah of Mahmoud Abbas – representing the "good Palestinians" – that has just announced through its al-Aqsa Martyrs Brigades – that it is joining the current armed struggle against Israel?

As unpleasant as it may be, we need to recognize that we are in a war with a bitter enemy that seeks our destruction and will use all means at its disposal – both military and diplomatic – to achieve its goals. It is supported by its people and their organizations – Fatah, Hamas, and Islamic Jihad. There is no concept of "peaceful inhabitants" in a war for Israel's survival – especially when they have been given repeated warnings to leave the schools, mosques, and playgrounds that Hamas and Islamic Jihad use as military bases in Gaza.

Let's start fighting a no-holds-barred war with no ceasefires and no negotiations. And when it's over and we are in full and absolute control of Gaza, then and only then, should we DICTATE THE TERMS of the peace according to the security needs and national self-interest of Israel.

Don't Just Shell Gaza: Liberate Gaza!

"We will yet return to Gush Katif!"

Sung by a large group of Israeli reservists
awaiting deployment into Gaza.

A t least four Israelis have been killed and several others seriously wounded in a mortar attack on a home in the Eshkol Regional Council, next to the Gaza border this afternoon. The wounded have been rushed to Soroka Hospital in Beersheba. The IDF is responding by vigorously shelling Hamas targets in Gaza.

While such a targeted murder of Israeli civilians should certainly be responded to, and responded to harshly, the war in Gaza can be waged much more effectively with a more proactive political/military approach that I believe Israel is ready for. In a recent survey, a whopping 87% of Israelis have expressed their support for the continuation of the operation. In fact, some unexpected prominent Cabinet members, like left-leaning Finance Minister Yair Lapid, have expressed a willingness to consider a broadening of the operation to include "reconquering" Gaza.

This would be a wise move for several reasons:

1. According to military intelligence experts, Gaza can only be effectively secured and demilitarized by full Israeli control of the region.

2. The Hamas and Islamic Jihad terrorist organizations would never agree to disarm as part of a negotiated agreement.

3.   Gaza is part of the historic Land of Israel, so a reassertion of Israeli authority over the region would be morally just, even if it's only done at first for tactical security reasons.

Once Israel fully reasserts its authority over Gaza, the wounds from the 2005 Israeli withdrawal from Gaza can finally begin to heal by allowing Jewish Israelis to once again build homes in Gush Katif, where Hamas missile launching pads have sadly taken the place of the once vibrant agricultural communities. Barring an official apology for the traumatic forced expulsion of 7,000 Jews from their homes, this would at least be seen as a tacit national admission that the withdrawal from Gaza was a tragic mistake.

This step-by-step approach should be taken by Israel's political leadership gradually, yet unapologetically, calmly explaining to the world the justice and the logic of each phase in the process. Will there be criticism? Certainly, but that is no reason not to go forward. The return to the historic Land of Israel has been fraught with great obstacles that are often not military, and critical world opinion is one such challenge.

May we be worthy of confronting and succeeding in meeting the challenges that lie ahead!

Yair Lapid On Gaza

"Self-reflection entails asking yourself questions about your values, assessing your strengths and failures, thinking about your perceptions and interactions with others, and imagining where you want to take your life in the future."

Bob Rosen, CEO Advisor, Author

Operation Protective Edge, the current war in Gaza, has revealed a remarkable consensus in Israel that the Hamas and Islamic Jihad terrorist attacks need to be ended once and for all. In the past, no such voices of support for such a war would have been heard on the left of the political spectrum. Such a case in point is Yair Lapid, the leader of the political party, Yesh Atid.

Lapid, you may recall, achieved nineteen seats in the last Knesset elections, more than any party other than Prime Minister Binyamin Netanyahu's Likud, by presenting his Yesh Atid as the latest and greatest centrist party in Israel. Despite this grand promo, the voices that have been heard in recent months, especially from his fellow MKs, have clearly been from the left of the political spectrum, and often quite vocal.

Therefore, it's very significant that in recent days, we've been hearing some rather surprising comments from the Yesh Atid chairman, calling for Israel to forcefully demilitarize Gaza and uncritically mentioning that the possibility of Israel "reconquering" Gaza is being discussed in the Cabinet. So the question needs to be asked – Is Lapid sincere and can he be trusted?

One MK from Yesh Atid told me some time ago that Lapid is a strong leader and an independent thinker who shouldn't be unfairly categorized as a leftist. I had actually been waiting for many months to see that maverick leader appear to the public, only to hear statement after statement from him praising Mahmoud Abbas of the Palestinian Authority and blasting "the settlers." True, this was most likely a frantic response to his ongoing fall in the polls, as an effort to bolster his left of center credentials and to prevent the drain-off to Tzipi Livni and to a resurgent Yitzhak Herzog's Labor party.

Nonetheless, it is certainly encouraging to see that Yair Lapid, and perhaps others, are now able to transcend the strange left-wing belief that war is always bad, and that the "Palestinians" are our partners in peace, not to mention the old and tired mantra that there is no military solution.

The current operation in Gaza is starting to prove that there is indeed a military solution and that we must take strong, uncompromising action to fulfill all of our objectives, from destroying all of the tunnels, to disarming the terrorists and asserting full Israeli control over Gaza. Then of course, we can start discussing how to reestablish and grow the Jewish civilian presence in Gaza in place of the missile launching pads that Hamas and Islamic Jihad had built on the ruins of those once-thriving Jewish communities. A permanent and significant Jewish presence is the most reliable way to ensure a permanent end to the rocket fire as well as to create long-term stability in that troubled southwestern corner of Israel.

Hillary Clinton's Moral Failure

"Sincerity – if you can fake that, you've got it made."

George Burns, American comedian

In an interview on Fusion TV, former US Secretary of State Hillary Clinton has once again attempted to show her firm grip of world affairs by responding to the repeated charges that Israel has been targeting schools, hospitals, and places of worship in its attacks on Gaza. The images of wounded child victims have been flashing on TV screens across America, usually accompanied by the words "war crimes." Unfortunately, many American politicians, rather than boldly refuting that canard, have been speaking out of both sides of their mouths, in a strange effort to be "even-handed."

"I'm not a military planner," Clinton said, "but ... Hamas puts its rockets, its missiles, in civilian areas – part of it is that Gaza's pretty small, and it's very densely populated." She went on to strongly urge a ceasefire "as soon as possible."

Sadly, the presumed front-running not yet candidate in the 2016 presidential elections is not yet ready to analyze the complexities of the Middle East. Her rather odd suggestion that the lack of space in Gaza is the reason why Hamas and Islamic Jihad use civilians as human shields would be laughable if it weren't so obscene. It raises serious doubts about Mrs. Clinton's knowledge, but more about her sincerity, when such a media-savvy politician doesn't recognize that missiles and rockets have intentionally been placed by Hamas and Islamic Jihad in many UN sponsored schools, and that tunnels have been built under homes, for the precise purpose of winning the Arab media war against Israel.

Using civilians, and especially children, as human shields is a war crime indeed, and most of the world not only remains silent, but actually blames Israel for attacking the terrorists who are intentionally hiding behind those civilians. Adding to the gravity of this scandal is the fact that the United Nations very well may be an accomplice to the crime, for how could they have been unaware that Hamas and Islamic Jihad were militarily active in their institutions?

In her recent public statements about Israel, Hillary Clinton has been doing a perverse balancing act between general expressions of support for Israel and an understanding and sympathy for the Arab Muslim narrative. Not only will justice not be served by such a failure of moral clarity, but there are political ramifications, as well. Such a lack of support for the moral correctness of Israel's struggle won't go over well with the majority of Americans that identify far greater with Israel than with Hamas, Islamic Jihad, and the rest of the so-called Palestinian people, whose leaders have fed them a love of terrorism with their mother's milk, along with a fierce hatred of Israel and Western civilization.

Is that who Hillary wants to pander to?

Israel: A Light Unto The Nations

"And unto your light, nations shall walk, and kings unto the brightness of your rising."

Isaiah 60:3

"I am the Lord; I called you with righteousness and I will strengthen your hand; I will protect you; I will set you for a covenant to the people, for a light to the nations."

Isaiah 42:6

I've been writing a lot about the war in Gaza – the bombings, the tunnels, the rockets, and the human shields, not to mention the political intrigue – but one important topic seems to be getting lost in the shuffle, and that is the remarkable nature of the people of Israel.

After 2,000 years of exile, during which time only a remnant had the privilege to live in the Land of Israel, albeit under adverse physical conditions, the Jewish people have come home from the four corners of thc Earth. Two thousand years of dwelling in other peoples' lands led to an enormous ethnic, religious, and cultural diversity in today's Israel, often leading to serious internal conflict on issues such as the military draft, defining acceptable social norms, and developing a Constitution that could possibly be made acceptable to all.

Despite all this, when the people of Israel are under attack, everyone bands together like a family in crisis. All other issues are put to the side and the success and welfare of our soldiers in their valiant struggle for Israel's survival becomes paramount. Teenagers spend much of their summer time performing volunteer projects, total strangers visit families that have lost children in the war and terrorism to comfort them, and neighbors inquire about the boys that they may know who have been wounded in the battle. The sense of caring beyond the call of duty is palpable among pedestrians in the street, in the bus stations, and on the train.

Much of the world is unaware that Israel is a tiny nation of eight million people, in a land barely the size of the American state of New Jersey, so the sense of family is still strong and the desire to help and to do good in times of crisis is paramount. From where does that sense of idealism derive? Perhaps it's a protective reaction or a rebellious streak, responding to a world that has been trying in vain to destroy us for thousands of years. Perhaps it's the optimism of our Torah, which says that we should always be trying to improve ourselves and to improve the world under God's leadership.

In any event, the behavior of the average Israeli in wartime is indeed a positive example for the entire world. The evil Israeli portrayed often by the Islamic propaganda machine around the world is a perverse caricature of the real Israeli, whose kindness shines through in difficult times.

These average Israelis are represented among all of the soldiers at the front, who are fighting the good fight for freedom against the Islamic tsunami, a tyranny that threatens not just Israel, but all of Western civilization. We just happen to be on the front lines. If we are successful, this too, will be a light unto the nations.

May we merit a speedy and complete victory!

The Fear Of Sovereignty

"The best defense is a good offense."

Unknown

It's a biblical story that I repeat often and that has enormous relevance to the present dilemma facing Prime Minister Binyamin Netanyahu and the Israeli Cabinet. When Joshua set up the Tabernacle, which preceded the Holy Temple, in Shiloh, thereby establishing it as Israel's capital city some 3,300 years ago, he spoke the following words to the Israelites, words that resonate to this very day:

> *"How long will you wait, before coming to take possession of the land that the Lord, God of your fathers has given you?"*
>
> Joshua 18:3

Joshua needed to say those words to the Israelis of that time, apparently because of their serious hesitation to take control of the difficult regions where enemies such as the Philistines were ensconced. The fear of entering costly wars in which many lives could have been lost, or the concern about applying sovereignty to a place where much of the population was hostile – These were all serious issues then as they are now, but Joshua reprimanded the people, urging them to go forward to claim their God-given lands, with faith in the justice of their cause.

In these perilous days for Israel, the Cabinet is discussing its next goals in the war in Gaza. Most Cabinet members seem to agree that Hamas and Islamic Jihad need to be disarmed, but there is less agreement about how to get the job done. Should Israel rely on a negotiated agreement that probably wouldn't be adhered to? Should it avoid a long stay in that troublesome coastal region?

It should by now be clear to all that only Israel can be counted on to disarm the terrorists, to bring them to their knees, and then to maintain the peace. Sadly, there is no other interested party that Israel can rely on to prevent the terrorist organizations from rearming with the help of their many friends, throughout the Islamic world and elsewhere.

Israeli Foreign Minister Avigdor Liberman's strange suggestion that the United Nations, those well-known lovers of the Jewish State, should be given a mandate over Gaza, is an especially horrifying prospect. That same UN that couldn't or wouldn't prevent Hamas weapons from being based in its own UNRWA schools in Gaza, or that oddly claimed that it didn't even know that the weapons were there – This is who Mr. Liberman wants to safeguard the peace in Gaza?

It's not easy and it's not pleasant to reject the advice of ostensible allies, but this is what Israel must do. Taking full control of Gaza and asserting Israel's sovereignty over the historic coastal region of Samson is the only way to keep the peace after the disarming of Hamas and Islamic Jihad, may it be accomplished speedily and completely.

As Joshua said to the Israelites, "Be strong and courageous, do not fear and do not lose resolve, for the Lord your God is with you ..."

Until The Next War

"I think that this is the first war in history that on the morrow the victors sued for peace and the vanquished called for unconditional surrender."

Abba Eban, Israel's Foreign Minister,
after Israel's decisive victory over
Arab armies in the 1967 Six Day War

Israel has a great army ... Dedicated soldiers committed to defending Israel and defeating her enemies ... Reservists who rush to the front at a moment's notice when called, with abundant eagerness to serve the country and to defend Israel.

This time was going to be different. This time the enemy would be soundly defeated and would be dealt a serious blow that they would never forget. The motivation of Israel's soldiers remained high throughout. Even though more than sixty soldiers were killed, and many others were wounded in battle, Israel's soldiers remained determined to defeat the enemy and to bring safety to Israel's citizens.

However, it appears that the politicians are going to snatch what should have been a military victory, yet again, out of the capable hands of the Israel Defense Forces, only to turn it into a political failure. Prime Minister Netanyahu spoke to the nation yesterday, as the last Israeli ground troops were leaving Gaza. He praised the defense minister and the soldiers for their efforts, emphasizing that the mission of destroying the Hamas and Islamic Jihad tunnels had been completed. True, a total of 32 tunnels near the Gaza border had been found and "neutralized," but many others remain operational under the populated cities of Gaza and near the

Egyptian border.

As the enemy rockets continue to be fired at Israeli cities, and after 48 hours of terrorist attacks in the streets of Jerusalem and beyond, Israel has agreed to a 72-hour ceasefire, while the Hamas, Islamic Jihad, and Fatah terrorists meet with the Egyptians, the UN, and the US to quickly iron out a long-term ceasefire agreement. No doubt such an agreement will be greatly publicized as an accomplishment that will "bring quiet," because it will include a provision stating that Hamas will halt rocket attacks on Israel.

If such an agreement is reached, what exactly will have been accomplished in this war? Was the purpose of the war just to return us to the situation that existed two years ago when the last war was ended prematurely? Was the purpose of this war just to destroy some of the tunnels and to get a promise to hold the fire for another year or two until the next war?

Unless Bibi Netanyahu suddenly learns to use the surprise factor in war and launches a sudden all-out military operation throughout Gaza to disarm Hamas and Islamic Jihad, it appears that this war is over. While no one in Israel actually likes war, there is a growing maturity, a growing understanding among the Israeli populace that when you fight a war, you need to fight to win and to win big. However, that understanding doesn't seem to have reached the politicians.

The main failure of Israel's current political leadership is in its ample ability to talk strong and to carry a big stick, but not to use it to the fullest extent possible, because of a lack of political courage to finish the job. There is the fear of having to continue responding to the unfair international criticism, as well as the fear of "the day after," of what to do with Gaza after its terrorists have been disarmed. Those are the questions that seem to haunt the mainstream politicians of Netanyahu's Likud party, including the boss himself, who seem to have abandoned the Zionist concept of asserting Jewish sovereignty over the Land of Israel. The terrorists of Hamas and Islamic Jihad in Gaza know this well, and therefore, they may temporarily stop the rocket fire as part of a long-term ceasefire arrangement in exchange for some Israeli concessions, but they will remain armed, they will restock their weapons supply, and yes, they will rebuild their tunnels. They also will remain in firm control of Gaza and will regroup, all the while strengthening their military forces.

Until the next war ...

Gaza: The Political Failure To Win

"Never give in, never give in, never; never; never; never – in nothing, great or small, large or petty – never give in except to convictions of honor and good sense."

Winston Churchill, British Statesman

D ateline November 2012: It was a humiliating spectacle.

All of Israel, not to mention the thousands of reservist soldiers amassed along the Gazan border, were waiting anxiously for the IDF ground offensive that would stop the Hamas rocket fire once and for all, but an unexpected press conference was held at which Prime Minister Binyamin Netanyahu, Foreign Minister Avigdor Liberman, and then Defense Minister Ehud Barak announced their quick acceptance of an Egyptian-brokered ceasefire arrangement, thus surrendering to international pressure before the ground operation had even begun.

Meanwhile, the streets of Gaza were filled with the haters of Israel celebrating the Israeli retreat with "victory candy" being handed out in the streets.

Is history repeating itself in 2014? Did we miss another opportunity to win a decisive victory, just like in 2012?

Now that it's clear that Prime Minister Binyamin Netanyahu and his Cabinet have decided to end Operation Protective Edge after several weeks on the battlefield, the attempts by the political echelon to post a victory sign on an inconclusive war will soon be clear and visible to all. In the coming days, we will be hearing political spin from all of the familiar spokespeople, which of course will include the PM himself, as well as his Defense Minister Moshe Yaalon and Netanyahu's loyal political ally, Minister of Intelligence Yuval Steinetz, telling us that Hamas suffered a crushing defeat.

When one looks at the stats, it appears that they are correct. On the battlefield, this was no replay of Israel's embarrassing retreat in 2012. In this year's war, the ground troops were sent in and performed heroically, and far more Gaza fighters and residents were killed than were Israelis. There also was extensive damage to thousands of terror targets and infrastructure in Gaza, far more than there was to Israeli towns and cities. Thirty-two known cross-border terror tunnels were destroyed.

Nonetheless, and the recent polls leave no doubt, the Israeli public was hoping for a decisive victory that would finish off Hamas and Islamic Jihad once and for all. At the height of the war, the calls for Israel to "demilitarize Gaza" and to "disarm the terrorists" were fast and furious and Bibi was among those making this a central political aim of the operation. Minister Steinetz spoke repeatedly about the need to retake control of Gaza, at least for an extended period of time in order to stop the rocket fire and to demilitarize Gaza.

That isn't what happened on the ground. Here are ten of the real results that indicate a pathetic lack of follow-through, which translates into a terrible failure at the political level:

1. Rather than suffering a knockout, Hamas remains on its feet – injured, but able to regroup, rearm, and prepare for the next battle.

2. Many tunnels remain intact, if not the 32 known ones that were "neutralized" near the Israeli border.

3. At least a third of the rockets, as well as many other weapons remain in the hands of Hamas and Islamic Jihad.

4. Once the supply lines into Gaza are opened as part of the long-term ceasefire deal, the flow of construction materials into Gaza will help to rebuild the terror tunnels.

5. The Hezbollah terrorist organization, which controls Lebanon, which has greater firepower than Hamas, and which is already reported to be building terror tunnels under the northern Israeli town of Metullah, will be greatly emboldened by our lack of political will to disarm Hamas.

6. Hamas and Islamic Jihad are receiving worldwide political legitimacy as a negotiating partner with Israel in Cairo.

7. US Secretary of State John Kerry will use the long-term ceasefire talks in Cairo as a springboard for "peace talks" with the Hamas-Fatah Palestinian Authority unity government.

8. The Hamas-Fatah Palestinian Authority will continue its push in international bodies to charge Israel with war crimes.

9. Israel will be investigated for war crimes at the UN, even though it is the Hamas, the Islamic Jihad, and the UN itself who should be charged with war crimes – for using and enabling the use of children as human shields.

10. Allowing Hamas and Islamic Jihad to remain on its feet will virtually ensure that we will be looking at a third Gaza war, in approximately another two years.

Prime Minister Netanyahu and his government missed a great opportunity, with massive public support, to finally destroy the monster that is Hamas and Islamic Jihad and to eliminate the danger from Gaza to Israel's citizens. Sadly, it has once again turned what could have been a great military victory into a political failure. Will we learn the lessons for next time?

Obama And The Palestinian Lie

"If you tell a big enough lie and tell it frequently enough, it will be believed."

Adolf Hitler, Nazi founder and leader

I t's quite rare to hear a comment about Israel from US President Barack Obama that I can actually agree with, but that comment was certainly made in yesterday's interview published in the New York Times.

Obama's First Comment:

"It is amazing to see what Israel has become over the last several decades. To have scratched out of rock this incredibly vibrant, incredibly successful, wealthy and powerful country is a testament to the ingenuity, energy and vision of the Jewish people."

I agree wholeheartedly, except for the part about our wealth that we don't yet have. The problem is that his remark was but a flowery prelude to a series of comments, given in response to a question, about pressuring Israel on the immoral and suicidal (for Israel) "land-for-peace formula." So while it was a generally positive statement, it was but a prelude for what followed.

Obama's Next Comment:

"If he (Prime Minister Binyamin Netanyahu) doesn't feel some internal pressure, then it's hard to see him making

> *some very difficult compromises, such as taking on the*
> *settler movement."*

Ah, yes, we all know about that problematic settler movement, those pesky troublemakers who have the "chutzpah" to insist on their right to live in Israel's historic biblical heartland, and who are always accused of stealing so-called Palestinian land from the Palestinian Arab country that never existed.

Finally, the Obama we have come to expect – pontificating about the rights of the Palestinians:

> *"You have to recognize that they have legitimate claims,*
> *and this is their land and neighborhood as well."*

Let's work backwards on this comment – Is this their neighborhood, as well? If we understand neighborhood to mean the Middle East as a whole, then it's true that the individuals who now call themselves "Palestinians" do, in fact, live in this neighborhood.

However – Is this their land and do they have legitimate claims to it? Absolutely not. Most of them came to the Land of Israel in the early part of the 20th century from other parts of the Middle East. They came looking for work in a growing economy that was being created solely by the enterprising, energetic Jewish people that Obama referred to, some of whom had been living here for generations, and many others who had returned to their formerly sovereign nation in the Land of Israel, soon to be reestablished as an independent nation in 1948.

No, Mr. Obama, while it's true that this land had been renamed "Palestina" by the Roman conquerors, who drove most of the Jews from their sovereign country 2,000 years ago, it was never again a sovereign country for any of the subsequent conquering colonists, nor for anyone, until the Jews finally returned to reestablish Israel.

As my Jerusalem-born father-in-law, an eighth generation Israeli, often reminds me, it is only the Jews of the Land of Israel who even used the term "Palestinians" to describe themselves. Many Jews living in the Land of Israel before 1948 were called Palestinian Jews, but the Arabs living in what was then known to the world as Palestine never accepted the moniker "Palestinian Arab," insisting that they were not Palestinians, but were instead an integral part of "the Arab nation."

The term "Palestinians" only reached its current usage about twenty years later when the Arabs realized that they needed to create an "underdog" in order to win the propaganda war against Israel, so they invented this new Palestinian people to refer only to Arabs, and usually to Arab Muslims. To further enhance the lie, and to increase their growing international political power, the Arabs nations and their fellow Jew-haters at the United Nations redefined the term to include all of the descendants of these neo-Palestinians, regardless of country of residence.

From there, the rest is history, but the claims of "legitimate rights" for a people that never existed historically, to a state that never existed historically, are absolutely and historically absurd.

Needless to say, the New York Times didn't inform President Obama of those uncomfortable historical facts.

Investigate The UN For War Crimes

"Peace will come when the Arabs will love their children more than they hate us."

Golda Meir, Israel's first female prime minister,
during a 1957 speech

I s the United Nations (UN) War Crimes Commission investigating the wrong party?

Canadian Foreign Affairs Minister John Baird has sharply criticized the choice of Canadian law professor William Schabas to head a United Nations commission examining possible war crimes against Israel in Gaza, citing past biases expressed by Schabas against Israel.

While Minister Baird deserves praise for standing with Israel against unfair criticism from a biased UN, the real problem is in the actual purpose of the investigation. Given the general facts that are known to every objective individual with a modicum of common sense, Israel is not the one that needs to be investigated. However, a commission does need to be established to get answers to several key questions:

Question One: Why were lethal weapons – including rockets – both stored and fired by Hamas and Islamic Jihad from United Nations Relief and Works Agency (UNRWA) schools?

Question Two: How is it possible that the UN had no advance knowledge that their children's schools were being used as weapons storage houses and missile launching pads?

Question Three: If the UN did know that its facilities were being used for such military purposes, why was such activity allowed?

Question Four: Knowing that there was a war going on, why was there apparently little or no care taken, not by the above organizations nor by the UN itself, for the safety of the children who attended those schools?

Using children as human shields is a war crime. The self-righteous officials at the UN seem to use the old Freudian defense mechanism of projection quite well, redirecting their own culpability by attacking their nemesis Israel. Perhaps the time has come for the UN to get off its US taxpayer-supported high horse and let itself be investigated for its own possible war crimes, at least as an accomplice with its buddies in Hamas and Islamic Jihad.

When will that commission be established?

Mahmoud Abbas: Our Reward For The Death Of 64 Soldiers

"President (Mahmoud) Abbas said ... during a meeting with Egyptian journalists and intellectuals in Cairo ... that the number of Martyrs (Shahids) from Hamas during the aggression against Gaza (i.e., Operation Protective Edge) was only 50, while 861 Martyrs fell from Fatah."

WAFA, official PA news agency

Now that the negotiations for a long-term ceasefire agreement between Israel and the Hamas-Fatah-Islamic Jihad triumvirate have taken center stage, the messianic peaceniks are once again pushing for the re-installment of Palestinian Authority (PA) President Mahmoud Abbas as the ruler in Gaza.

Former President of Israel, Shimon Peres, as a heavily-invested shareholder in the failed "peace process," continues to be a prime catalyst on the Left for the re-crowning of Abbas, proclaiming that he is a "partner for peace."

Despite his retirement from the ceremonial post of President, Peres continues to use his bully pulpit to pressure Israel to sign a deal with Hamas that would hand the proverbial keys of Gaza over to Abbas and his Fatah terrorists. This approach, so the theory goes, would have Gaza run by the peace-seeking moderates led by Abbas, as opposed to the violent Hamas and Islamic Jihad terrorists.

Unfortunately, this theory, which seems to be strongly adhered to by the "Kerryites" in Washington, boldly rivals the "Flat-Earth" theory in its abysmally low level of sophistication. All that one needs to do is to take a quick peek at the proud assertions on the Fatah Facebook page, in order to be disabused of the old and tired peaceful Fatah theory:

> *Listen well! To whoever does not know Fatah and argues with this giant movement:*
>
> *Fatah has killed 11,000 Israelis; Fatah has sacrificed 170,000 Martyrs (Shahids) ...*
>
> *Fatah was the first to carry out operations (i.e., terror attacks) during the first Intifada ...*
>
> *Fatah was the first to fight in the second Intifada (i.e., PA terror campaign 2000-2005) ...*
>
> *Fatah led the Palestinian attacks on Israel in the UN ...*
>
> *Fatah leads the peaceful popular resistance against Israel ... Stop and think before you attack (Fatah).*

For an entire month, Israel's brave youth fought valiantly in the difficult tunnels and alleyways of Gazan cities, with 64 courageous soldiers losing their lives, and with hundreds of others wounded.

Did those 64 young men die in vain, all for the purpose of reinstating Mahmoud Abbas as king of Gaza?

Are these obsequious Abbas groupies aware that Abbas's PA pays all of the terrorists' salaries for their attacks on Israeli civilians?

Are these sanctimonious, "Peresitic" peaceniks who fawn over "the good terrorists" aware that the PA is an equal opportunity employer – that the salaries go not just to Fatah terrorists, but also to the terrorists of Hamas and Islamic Jihad? Has Abbas also begun funding, hence encouraging, the terrorism of the notorious Islamic State group that is reported to now be active in Gaza?

Throughout the war in Gaza, the Fatah-Hamas unity government has been held together, with its alliance against Israel firmly intact and even strengthened. Despite their slight differences in strategy and public image, could it be that they actually share the goal of destroying Israel?

Tel Aviv's Sabbath Day: Religious Coercion?

"Sabbath observance invites us to stop. It invites us to rest. It asks us to notice that while we rest, the world continues without our help. It invites us to delight in the world's beauty and abundance."

Wendell Berry, conservationist, farmer, English professor

Israel's Sabbath day, otherwise known as the Shabbat or Shabbos, depending on who's talking about it, is once again stirring up controversy in the stores and the streets of Tel Aviv. What is this fuss all about and why should we care?

"Observe the Sabbath day to keep it holy."

Deuteronomy 5:12

Nice biblical words, and much of the Israeli public takes those words very seriously, but what about the large part of the public that doesn't believe in it, or believes in it only partially? Shouldn't they be allowed to shop to their hearts' content on Saturday afternoon? Why should their freedom be restricted by forced store closures?

In Israel's capital city of Jerusalem, there is hardly a supermarket or grocery store open on Shabbat. This is partially because of the municipal bylaws making such activity prohibitive, but also because of the very large religiously observant population, most of whom desire the peaceful feeling of walking through the streets without the noise of heavy commercial activity, but many of whom also want the Sabbath to be a symbolic standard for the nation of Israel and sincerely believe that the nation would be strengthened, as it says in the Torah, by such public observance.

However, much of the staunchly secular population vigorously objects, seeing such laws as coercive. For example, the city of Tel Aviv has always been known as "the free city," with its extensive nightlife and its assertive flaunting of vices.

How can the municipality inflict Shabbat grocery closures on such a lively population?

The truth is that it always has, to some extent. The city of Tel Aviv has always had bylaws enforcing some degree of public Sabbath observance. Cafes are open on Shabbat, but fines are issued to supermarkets and grocery stores that open their doors for business on Shabbat. Is it an infringement of public freedom?

Well, yes, it certainly seems to be. While the religious public would strongly argue that Shabbat observance actually frees us to spend quiet, reflective time with our families, away from the hustle-bustle of the shopping and the markets, the truth is that it is a restriction of free choice.

However, there is another angle that has inadvertently been highlighted by recent attempts in Tel Aviv at changing the bylaws to allow groceries to be open on Shabbat – the right of those who are employed in such businesses to a day of rest. Isn't it also a restriction of freedom to compel someone to work?

Even so, the commercial engine is not so easily silenced. There has been a growing phenomenon of large grocery chains in Tel Aviv opening on Shabbat. Ignoring municipal bylaws, they swallow the fines and open up for full business, knowing that they are large enough to withstand the penalty.

This has sparked a new, and perhaps unexpected form

of protest against coercion. This past Friday, a contingent of small business owners of grocery stores in Tel Aviv flocked to the larger chain stores, handing out mock violation notices, protesting their opening for business as usual on Shabbat, which they described as unfair and discriminatory competition. The small grocery store owners pointed out that the current arrangement puts them at a disadvantage against the big chains, which can afford to keep their stores staffed on Shabbat. Small business owners, they say, deserve a day off, too.

As one small store owner explained it, "We favor a free Tel Aviv – this city has always been free and open and it should stay that way, but this city cannot continue retail trade that so sweepingly and plainly robs me and my friends of the one free day in the week, which everyone in the city deserves."

And that quote reveals an often ignored perspective, which in turn reveals a critical universal aspect in the nature of the Shabbat, a day of rest for all. As slaves in Egypt, we were forced to endure a grueling, merciless workload with little regard for human needs. The Shabbat is, indeed, a day of freedom from a full seven days of labor, or an excessively grueling work week with no respite, what is known in modern parlance as "the rat race." In this sense, what appears on the surface to be a demand for total freedom from religious coercion can actually be an obstruction of freedom.

Yes, the return to the land as a sovereign nation has often required a difficult rethinking of the question of how to live together peacefully, productively, and in a way that is consistent with the wonderful heritage of Israel. In our internal conflicts, we Israelis tend to see things in black and white, but the reality is often not as it seems.

To be an Israeli is to struggle with these issues and to seek peaceful solutions, and to do so, as difficult as it often is, working together as a people.

This complex return to the land is certainly unique in the annals of humanity, and it's not always easy, but after 2,000 years of being scattered around the world, persecuted, and killed by the millions, it's also a privilege.

The "Islamic State" Wake-Up Call

"We do not know whether Hitler is going to found a new Islam. He is already on the way; he is like Muhammad. The emotion in Germany is Islamic; warlike and Islamic. They are all drunk with a wild god."

Carl Jung, Swiss founder of analytical psychology

The "Islamic State" terrorist group active in Iraq, in Syria, and even in Gaza, has sounded a wake-up call to the West to arise from its slumber. The message should be clear – The Islamic threat is based on a greater ideology, which happens to be the dominant one in Islam as it is practiced today, and is not specific to any one group or organization. Are world leaders listening?

When US President Barack Hussein Obama entered office in January of 2009, all efforts were made to refrain from using the expression "Islamic terrorism." In fact an order was given to all members of his administration that no longer would the term be used. Specifically, they would refer only to al-Qaeda terrorism or Taliban terrorism and be abundantly cautious not to blame Islam for this phenomenon of terrorism. Incredibly, the root cause of the terrorism, the ideology from which Muslims learn the concept of Jihad, or Holy War against non-Muslims, would be ignored. As I explained in my book "The Islamic Tsunami: Israel and America in the Age of Obama," terrorism did not evolve in a vacuum, but grew naturally from an ideology that, at least in practice, considers Jihad to be the highest precept that a Muslim can aspire to.

Given that basic understanding, should we be surprised

that the Muslims chant, "Allah Hu Akhbar," which actually means "Allah is greater," when carrying out terrorist attacks? Should we be surprised that Muslims chant those same words when they chase Jews off the Temple Mount in Jerusalem or when the Islamic State terrorists take Christians and other non-Muslims as sex-slaves in Syria and Iraq? We're afraid to face that reality, but Jihadist philosophy is part and parcel of their core "religious" belief system.

Are there Muslims who don't share these beliefs? Yes, there are, but they are rare and most are terrified to speak out against the Jihadists, who clearly are the dominant trend in Islam and who threaten any Muslim who dares to speak out against them. It is incorrect and cowardly to repeatedly speak of "Radical Islam," as if it is some fringe ideology. The Jihadists are the core of Islam, which is radical! I wish that were not the case, but how else do we explain the stunning rise in the last few decades of Islamic State, Hezbollah, Hamas, Fatah, al-Aqsa Martyrs Brigades, Taliban, al-Qaeda, Boko Haram, and Islamic Jihad, along with the Ayatollahs of Iran? In no other religion is there such a frightening, cancerous growth that threatens the entire world with its violent, hatred of "the other."

The threat of the "Islamic State" and its rapid and very vocal growth in the Middle East is not just that of a particular group or a particular brand of "extreme" Sunni Islam, nor is the nuclear threat from Iran just the threat of a particular brand of "extreme" Shiite Islam. The Persian Gulf "moderates" in Qatar and Saudi Arabia heavily fund their favorite Islamic terrorists, as well.

The bottom line is that the Jihadist threat to the non-Muslim world crosses all ethnic and denominational boundaries and threatens to engulf all of what they call "the unbelievers" in a great Islamic Tsunami. And that should concern all of us.

Vacillation Brings Defeat

"Victory at all costs, victory in spite of all terror, victory however long and hard the road may be; for without victory, there is no survival."

Winston Churchill, British Statesman

Three clear orders were issued by Hamas kingpin Khaled Mashal in the last 48 hours:

1.   Attempt to overthrow the Fatah faction of the Palestinian Authority in Judea and Samaria (the so-called West Bank).

2.   Increase the planning of terrorist attacks on Israeli civilians in Judea and Samaria and other parts of Israel.

3.   Renew the launching of rockets from Gaza at Israel's citics.

There is no doubt that this burst of aggressive orders has contributed to the collapse of the latest ceasefire, and that was likely Mashal's intention, but the most important thing we can learn from all this is the importance of decisiveness. As evil as he is in his Muslim Brotherhood-Hamas brand of fanaticism, Mashal provides clear leadership, and that is one of the reasons he has managed to maintain his leadership from his base in Qatar, despite his distance from the core conflict and Hamas's terrorist stronghold in Gaza.

Closer to home, Prime Minister Binyamin (Bibi) Netanyahu and his sidekick Defense Minister Moshe (Bogie) Yaalon, after days of hesitation, sent in thousands of ground troops about a month ago to destroy the terror tunnels that had been found close to the border with Israel, while leaving many others intact. Once those 32 tunnels were methodically destroyed, the ground troops were immediately withdrawn and the tens of thousands of reservists were sent home, as if the entire job had been completed.

But many tunnels remained and many rockets remained and many weapons remained. In short, the Hamas/Islamic Jihad terror infrastructure in Gaza remains intact and, according to recent polls, most of the Israeli public does not feel that the job was completed.

Since the withdrawal of the ground troops, the Prime Minister has been the epitome of indecisiveness, allowing Mashal and his Hamas terrorists to firmly dictate the rules of the game. Bibi has quickly agreed to almost every ceasefire proposal, then waited with bated breath to see if Uncle Khaled will accept our desire to stop fighting. If Uncle Khaled decides instead to punish Bibi and Bogie by firing rockets at Israel's cities, the pathetic Bibi and Bogie duo, rather than providing strong leadership for the IDF, responds with oh-so carefully pinpointed air attacks on Hamas terrorists in Gaza. The vacillating politicians, despite their occasional bold public statements and threats of "firm retaliation," seem to be frightened that some Hamas/Islamic Jihad civilians might get killed and that the terror-compliant UN might accuse Israel of "war crimes" or that Obama and Kerry will deliver another pompous lecture to us about "morality," as the American air force ruthlessly bombs the Islamic State terrorists in Iraq.

Prime Minister Netanyahu was elected to provide leadership. As unsettling as it may be for Israel's citizens, all of whom have soldiers in their families, the reservists need to be brought back to the front and an all-out war needs to be carried out until the white flags of surrender replace the green Hamas flags that are flying over the buildings in Gaza. Not one weapon should remain in their hands.

If Bibi's fear of hurting the non-uniformed enemy in wartime is too great, if his fear of defying the Obama administration is too great, if his fear of the admittedly messy business of disarming Hamas and Islamic Jihad is too great, and if his fear of retaking control of Gaza is too great, then he should step aside and let the voters choose a replacement who is not afraid to do the job.

The age in which vacillation and pathetic hesitation is an option for the reestablished State of Israel has passed. Dilly-dallying back and forth at the whims of Khaled Mashal won't win the war, but it will prolong this embarrassing game of tit-for-tat that we are allowing Mashal to dictate. The Hamas-Islamic Jihad-Fatah triumvirate knows well that it would be crushingly defeated in an all-out no-holds-barred war with Israel, so they prefer to drag it out as a sick game of kidnappings, ceasefires, targeted killings, and rocket fire.

Israel needs strong, decisive leadership. Netanyahu's legacy will be determined by how he leads Israel in defeating its enemies, starting now with Hamas and ending with soon to be nuclear Iran and its Hezbollah proxy in Lebanon. Bibi, go forward – hard and fast. The courage to take decisive action is sorely needed, with a clear eye on the disarming of the terrorist organizations and the full repossession of Gaza. Let the hypocritical world scream and shout, because they will do so in any event. The people of Israel and the God of Israel will stand with you.

Bibi And The Politics Of Weakness

"Every day, my daddy told me the same thing. 'Once a task is just begun, never leave it till it's done. Be the labour great or small, do it well or not at all.' "

Quincy Jones, musician

Prime Minister Binyamin (Bibi) Netanyahu's signing of the long-term ceasefire agreement with the Islamic terrorist leadership of Hamas, Islamic Jihad, and Fatah raises serious questions, and not just about war and peace.

The image of Netanyahu in the West is that of a "hard-nosed," tough, right-wing leader, who is uncompromising when it comes to asserting Israel's claim to what the world media calls "greater Israel," more accurately defined and translated from the Hebrew as "the complete Land of Israel." He is revered by Israel's supporters around the world as a bold defender of Israel, as he confronts often hostile news anchors around the world, and in perfect English no less.

Notwithstanding his strong communication skills, the reality on the ground is quite different. Everyone in Israel knows that Bibi is very susceptible to pressure, especially when it comes from an American administration that has broken new records for hostility towards Israel. The agreement to repeated ceasefires, which in effect tied the hands of the Israel Defense Forces in the Gaza conflict, was a result of such pressure and Netanyahu's inability, despite occasional tough talk, to stand up to that pressure.

Is that the only reason that he caved and agreed to a

ceasefire in Gaza that doesn't provide security to the residents of the Gaza belt communities nor to the cities of the South? Is American pressure the only reason why he agreed to a ceasefire that leaves the Hamas infrastructure damaged, but intact? The motivation of our soldiers to sacrifice their personal safety for the sake of the homeland had never been higher. Was it all in vain?

Sadly, Bibi's submission to pressure is apparently matched by his lack of Zionist conviction when it comes to the entire Land of Israel. Despite his upbringing in a home of complete Land of Israel Zionists, his support over the years for Israel's development of Judea, Samaria, Gaza, and eastern Jerusalem has been less than stellar, to say the least. The only time we ever see Netanyahu in Samaria is during an election campaign when he comes to plant symbolic trees, only to have those trees symbolically uprooted months later with the obstruction of construction in these communities, or even worse, the expulsion of young families from idealistic hilltop communities. Every resident in the established communities here in Samaria can tell you that the demand for homes is much greater than the supply. The lack of building permits, which have to be authorized by the defense minister, is the reason. Undoubtedly, Netanyahu's lack of determination to enable growth in the biblical heartland extends all the more so to his apparent lack of belief in our historical right to reassert our authority in Gaza.

Despite his wishy-washy behavior in leading the Gaza battle as Commander-in-Chief, Prime Minister Netanyahu has actually taken a bold political gamble by agreeing to this long-term ceasefire. Knowing that half of his Security Cabinet would oppose such a pathetic deal, which doesn't even return the bodies of the two dead Israeli soldiers that remain in enemy hands, he used a technicality to approve the deal without a vote. Thus, he will have to take full political responsibility for the consequences, as Hamas and Islamic Jihad will immediately begin the process of rebuilding, restocking, and rearming, all in preparation for the next war.

Returning To The
Old/New Political Battleground

"Let me define a leader. He must have vision and passion and not be afraid of any problem ..."

A.P.J. Abdul Kalam, President of India, scientist

I t seems clear and apparent to all that the Gaza ceasefire agreement is now in place, which will lead to an approximately 1-2 year period of relative calm in the Negev.

That is the likely scenario, at least until Hamas has rebuilt, rearmed, and is ready for the next war. It's certainly not unreasonable to assume that they will be joined at that time by their Fatah partners in the Palestinian Authority (PA), who will have seen that their diminished standing among the non-uniformed terrorists, AKA – the majority of the so-called Palestinian people – requires them to be an active part of the violent "resistance," not just in words, but also in more than sporadic terror action. We can also expect that once that war returns, Hamas and Fatah will have the active support of Islamic Jihad and perhaps The Islamic State (ISIS), unless a new, glamorously Jihadist, and even more radical offshoot of al-Qaeda will have emerged by then.

Meanwhile, the political battleground is likely to return to the biblical heartland of Judea and Samaria, the notorious "West Bank," and eastern Jerusalem, as the Hamas-Fatah unity PA brings its demand for a Palestinian State comprising those regions to the United Nations (UN) Security Council and to the International Criminal Court (ICC).

That is why this morning's announcement that Israel will approve the transfer of 4,000 dunams (nearly 1,000 acres) of land in the Gush Etzion section of Judea to Israeli state control is at least symbolically significant. Yes, any transfer of land to official Israeli control has to pass a proper legal process, and Prime Minister Netanyahu and his Likud party dominated governments haven't been supporting such land transfers in recent years, but now is the time to move in that direction – to assert our rights to the land.

With all due respect to Gaza, which will ultimately be returned to Israeli control and will eventually be reestablished as a thriving part of the State of Israel, the political struggle for the Land of Israel will clearly be won in the biblical heartland, where the most historical cities that we read about in the Torah, in the Bible, are located. The region of Gush Etzion, on the southern edge of Bethlehem, was reestablished shortly after Israel's miraculous Six Day War in 1967, when Judea, Samaria, eastern Jerusalem, Sinai, Gaza, and the Golan Heights were liberated by the army of Israel. It's worthwhile to remember that the IDF, fighting ferociously, with seemingly inexplicable passion and emotion, won the war in six days and on the seventh day they rested. In that particular case, the UN-brokered ceasefire was only agreed to by Israel after those historically and strategically vital regions had been fully recaptured. The Almighty had given us a great opportunity and we seized the moment. Eventually, the politicians, true to form, betrayed that opportunity by handing over the Temple Mount, and eventually Sinai and Gaza to our enemies.

Some 47 years later, most of Judea and Samaria remains in our hands, even though seven Arab-occupied cities and some Jewish communities have been handed over to the Palestinian Authority, which was established after the Oslo "Peace" Agreements were inked near the end of 1993. Since those politically horrific days, we have seen some of the worst waves of terrorism in Israel's history.

Few people continue to share the wild-eyed, even blind optimism of a Shimon Peres, who pushed that process, and who irresponsibly still proclaims his imaginary vision of a new Middle East in the age of peace. However, a new kind of realistic optimism has reemerged, as we have seen a trend in the Israeli public that has been exploring and gradually reconnecting to its biblical roots and Jewish tradition. As the rest of Western civilization has been moving away from tradition, family, and biblical heritage, Israel is moving towards it in a big way. This trend can only make Israel stronger in defense of its beloved Land of Israel that the historical, reestablished towns in Samaria, Judea, and Jerusalem represent.

As our enemies go to the UN and the ICC with their false claims that we are occupying their "country," which in fact never existed and never had a right to exist, this would be an opportune time for Israel's political leadership to enable Jews to once again build and buy homes in the biblical heartland, The unofficial semi-freeze on the issuing of construction permits for Jews, along with the unreasonable bureaucratic restrictions that have hampered our natural growth, are immoral and politically foolish. Let's start building again.

Netanyahu And Abbas:
Self-Destructive Bedfellows

"An appeaser is one who feeds a crocodile – hoping it will eat him last."

Winston Churchill, British Statesman

Have Israeli Prime Minister Binyamin (Bibi) Netanyahu and Palestinian (PA) Chairman Mahmoud Abbas been in bed together to their own mutual detriment?

While the analogy might be a bit distasteful, it certainly represents the gravity of the situation. It has been revealed that at the height of the Gaza ceasefire negotiations, Netanyahu and Abbas held a secret pow-wow in Jordan to discuss a variety of issues. This despite the Hamas-Fatah unity government, established against Netanyahu's warnings; this despite Abbas's repeated threats to accuse Israel of war crimes at the International Criminal Court (ICC), and despite his insistence on demanding that the United Nations (UN) Security Council force Israel to retreat to the 1949 armistice lines, or to what Netanyahu has correctly referred to as "the indefensible 1967 borders."

This cavorting with the enemy takes place on the backdrop of an unofficial building freeze imposed by Netanyahu on the Jewish residents of Judea and Samaria (the so-called West Bank). It was recently announced that there has been a 76% drop in building starts in the Jewish communities of these heartland regions in the first quarter of 2014. This is not for lack of public desire or public demand for housing. While

Netanyahu has been bending over backwards to provide "economic peace" through massive financial aid to the PA-controlled areas, thereby fattening the wallet of the average Arab resident in Judea and Samaria, many hundreds of Jewish families with many children are forced to remain for years in caravans, or two-room no-frills trailer homes, due to the serious shortage of housing in the Jewish communities.

Yet the partnership continues. As Abbas repeatedly violates past agreements, such as the Oslo Accords, with his Hamas-Fatah unity government; as the PA continues to incite and to teach its children that Jews are Nazis; as Abbas repeatedly spits in his face, Bibi meekly wipes it off and then returns to the well-mannered, well-spoken Jew-hater for another civilized secret meeting followed by more public abuse of Israel.

It's interesting to note that, according to the Palestinian Center for Policy and Survey Research poll reported today by the Associated Press, if presidential elections were held today in the PA unity government, Hamas leader Ismail Haniyeh would receive a whopping 62% of the vote, while Fatah's Abbas would receive a humiliating 32%. In an almost simultaneous poll of the Israeli public by Channel Two, rating Israel's political leadership, it was reported that Netanyahu's approval rating has plummeted down to – you guessed it – 32%.

Yes, Jewish history makes for strange bedfellows, but we have seen that those leaders who pander to Israel's enemies or trade off parts of our God-given homeland, as if it's a mundane part of a jigsaw puzzle, eventually lose power. As we approach Rosh Hashanah, the Jewish New Year, our traditional time of reflection and self-improvement, Netanyahu should pay close attention to this lesson of history and start thinking seriously about abandoning the PA snake as he continues his free-fall drop in public support. At least with Hamas and Islamic Jihad, there are no illusions. The entire political spectrum in Israel knows that they are the enemy. Such a shift wouldn't just help Bibi politically, but would certainly be a wise and prescient move for the good of the nation. And that's good politics.

Beheadings:
Learning From The Founder Of Islam

"America and Islam are not exclusive, and need not be in competition. Instead, they overlap, and share common principles of justice and progress, tolerance and the dignity of all human beings."

US President Barack Obama

"We (Muslims) will conquer the world; so that 'there is no God but Allah, and Muhammad is the Prophet of Allah' will be triumphant over the domes of Moscow, Washington, and Paris ... We will annihilate America."

Iraqi Ayatollah Ahmad Husseini Al-Baghdadi

The political leadership of the Western world, obviously including the current resident of the White House, has long sought to find accommodation with the Islamic world, despite, or perhaps because of, all of the threats emanating from it. Has it been an exercise in futility?

The Islamic State (IS or ISIS) phenomenon, as represented in the recent gruesome beheadings of American journalists, has sent shock waves throughout Western civilization on a level unrivaled since the World Trade Center attacks of 9/11. The troubling questions being asked by many, and summarized below, reveal the deep confusion about how to respond:

1. What drives individuals to cut off other people's heads?

2. How does someone who grew up in the freedom of the USA or UK choose to become an active member of such a radical Islamic group?

3. Can this fanaticism actually be motivated by a great religion like Islam, or is it just Radical Islam?

To understand the Islamic State phenomenon, one needs to go to the root of Islam, or its founder, Muhammad, who 1,400 years ago established a new religion.

Muhammad was an angry young orphan, mostly raised by his uncle Abu Talib, a textile merchant who would often travel on camel caravans to other lands, taking his nephew with him. It was on these travels with his uncle that young Muhammad learned about different cultures and religions. As he was illiterate, this knowledge was acquired solely by listening to stories and oral traditions about Judaism, Christianity, Zoroastrianism, and the various Arabian pagan religions that were prevalent at that time. He eventually would adopt bits and pieces of all of these in creating his new religion, even trying to lure them to his new religion by appealing to certain key beliefs, such as briefly advocating the Jewish practice of facing Jerusalem in prayer. When his claims of prophecy were rejected by the Jews, among others, he officially established the direction of prayer away from Jerusalem, to Mecca.

After Muhammad's painful rejection by the Jews and Christians of that time, as well as by many pagan Arabs in Mecca, he fled to Medina, where he officially established his religion in the year 622. Some of his followers, who, unlike their leader, were literate, began to write down his sayings and stories, which eventually evolved into the Sura and the Hadith, the written Koran and the written oral tradition, based on the example set by Muhammad of how to lead a proper life.

Muhammad's life is known to Muslims as "the Sunna," which means "the usual practice" or "the example." In Islamic terminology, it refers to the life and ways of Muhammad. In other words, the Muslims have always looked to the life of Muhammad for guidance as to how to relate to other people and other nations. For this information, Muslims look to the Sura, which is the main text of the Koran, or to the Hadith, which is the written version of the Muslim oral tradition, consisting mainly of what Muslims consider to be the valuable lessons about how to live life, according to "the prophet."

This is the key to understanding the Islamic mentality, as well as the Islamic State (or IS or ISIS) organization that is chopping off heads. The philosophy of Jihad, or holy war against what Muhammad called "the unbelievers," is central in Islam. This is an obligation upon every Muslim, and the "holy" Islamic texts of the Koran and Hadith are replete with verses exhorting the faithful to make violent, holy war against the "unbelievers," and specifically the Jews and the Christians, who had rejected Muhammad's false claims of prophecy.

> *"When you meet the infidels in the battlefield, strike off their heads."*
>
> Sura 47:4

The beheadings of Western journalists, as frightening as they are, are nothing as compared to the savagery that Muhammad advocated, and in fact carried out.

In the year 627, Muhammad and his warriors laid siege around the Jewish tribe known as the "Banu Qurayzah" in Medina. He ordered the construction of trenches around the city. Ibn Ishaq, Islam's earliest biographer of Muhammad, describes what happened next:

"Then they (Banu Qurayzah) surrendered ... then he sent for them and struck off their heads in those trenches as they were brought out to them in batches ... They were 600 or 700 in all, though some put the figures as high as 800 or 900 ... This went on until the apostle made an end to them."

When the Islamic State monsters behead Western journalists, they are simply following the example of "The Sunna." This is not some offshoot of Islam called "Radical Islam" or "Islamism." The Jihad and the beheadings come straight from the core of Islam, which is radical.

Not every Muslim is a violent Jihadist, but the few Muslims who are opposed to them are usually afraid to speak out, for fear of their lives.

It's absolutely vital that we remember that those American Muslims or British Muslims who join Islamic State are simply following "The Sunna." By doing so, they are adhering to a sick ideology that is more dangerous than Nazism or Communism ever were, because it claims to be a religion, and therefore, people in the West, who believe in freedom of religion, don't know how to confront it.

But confront it they must, for if they don't, they will soon find themselves drowning in this ferocious Islamic tsunami of hatred, intolerance, and death. And then it will be too late.

Why Are The Muslims
Denouncing Islamic State?

"ISIL (Islamic State of Syria and the Levant) is not Islamic."

US President Barack Obama

The lightning rise of the Islamic State (IS or ISIS or ISIL) terrorist group, with their shocking beheadings of American journalists and mass rapes and enslavement of women and children has greatly disturbed the apathy of the free world and, most likely, forced it to take unexpected action.

What is more surprising, however, is the eager rush of some of the worst terror-supporting nations in the Islamic world, countries like Iran and Saudi Arabia, to either officially or unofficially join the burgeoning American-led coalition preparing to attack ISIS in a big way. Remember – these are nations that routinely cut off the hands of shoplifters, that don't allow women to drive, and/or sentence to death a Muslim who changes his religion. Beheadings are not unheard of in these countries, and are considered to be an acceptable form of punishment, especially since Muhammad, the founder of Islam, is known (from Islamic sources) to have proudly beheaded between 600-900 Jews in one day.

Despite the not-so-grand tradition of beheadings in the Islamic world, the Islamic State phenomenon has threatened the entrenched regimes in the Middle East with its rapid rise to power, as well as its openly stated desire to establish an Islamic Caliphate, leading to worldwide Islamic rule under its leadership. The idea of an Islamic Caliphate is one that few believing Muslims would object to in theory, but presumably, this ISIS-led crusade would not honor the leadership of the royal family of Saudi Arabia, which is generally happy to support terrorism, as long as it doesn't threaten the kingdom's rule and its vast oil proceeds.

Ah, but this Islamic State group is different – fighting for Allah with a fierce passion and no-holds barred fanaticism and belief in the righteousness of its cause – with little regard for the interests of the corrupt despots in the broader Islamic world. Even the ideological Ayatollahs of Iran, staunch supporters of global terrorism and enemies of both "the Great Satan" (the USA) and "the Little Satan" (Israel) aren't pure enough in the eyes of Islamic State, and besides, the Ayatollahs are of the rival Shiite Muslims, as opposed to the Sunni fighters of the Islamic State.

The internal Islamic rivalries have long baffled the Western world, which tends to see things through the eyes of freedom of speech, freedom of religion, and equal rights. The Islamic world is firmly based on the principle of Jihad, or holy war against what it calls the unbelievers.

The real question is not whether the Muslim leaders will support Jihad, as expressed by the terrorist acts carried out against Israel, the USA, the UK, and other free countries. All believing Muslims must support, at least secretly or passively, anything that they think will eventually lead to the destruction of both Israel and the United States and to the weakening and eventual elimination of Western, or Judeo-Christian civilization. This is straight from the doctrine of the Muslim Brotherhood, which calls for a "Jihadist process to destroy and eliminate the Western civilization from within." The Muslim Brotherhood may often use non-violent means to achieve the same goals as their more radical Muslim brothers in Islamic State, which currently uses brutal violence and public humiliation, but the goals are the same.

There is, however, one element in this complex situation that trumps all, and that is self-interest. The royal family in Saudi Arabia wants to maintain its perceived role as the leader of Sunni Islam, as well as the esteemed guardian of the holy places in Mecca, and they certainly do not want to be dominated by Islamic State. Similarly, the Ayatollahs of Iran are proud leaders of Shiite Islam and aspiring leaders of all Muslims. They are also primary sponsors of the Hezbollah and Hamas terrorist organizations, as well as feverishly pursuing the nuclear bomb with the ability to destroy Israel, but not only Israel.

These nations do not want to lose their power, nor do they want to lose their dominant roles, and if the United States-led coalition has the potential to cut the Islamic State down to size, then they will be in favor and will lend their support, if not their troops. Despite the nefarious goals that are shared by all of these Islamic players, all believing in the Islamic revolution and an eventual worldwide Islamic Caliphate, self-interest comes first. And that is what will determine the Middle East battles in the coming weeks and months.

The Sisi Savior Sinai Solution

"We are believers, the children of believers, and we have no one to rely on other than our Father in Heaven ..."

Sung by Israeli soldiers entering the battle in Gaza

E gyptian President Abdel Fattah al-Sisi is denying the by now widespread reports of the peace plan that he proposed during the Gaza ceasefire negotiations. The plan reportedly offered the Palestinian Authority (PA) 160 square kilometers (100 square miles) of the Sinai Desert adjacent to Gaza, which together with Gaza could be a decent-sized, demilitarized, independent Palestinian state.

The plan would also continue the current autonomy arrangement in the PA-run cities in Judea and Samaria (the so-called West Bank). It has been reported that Abbas rejected the offer outright. Nonetheless, the question that everyone is now asking is – Did Sisi make the offer or didn't he?

Since Sisi's offer is now being vehemently denied by PA Chairman/President Mahmoud Abbas and by Sisi, as well as their advisors, we probably won't get an answer to that question, at least not right away, but we can certainly learn a lot from the various reactions to the reported plan. Let's sum up those reactions right here:

Abbas: "No such plan exists. Anyhow, I would never agree to any plan that doesn't include the pre-1967 borders – the West Bank (Judea and Samaria) plus al-Quds (Jerusalem) as the capital of our independent State of Palestine."

Sisi: "No such plan exists. I would never suggest such a plan and I don't have the authority to suggest such a plan."

Right-Wing MKs: "It's about time that an important Arab nation, or any nation for that matter, made a constructive proposal that can be a basis for resolving the conflict."

What do I think? Aside from the misguided attempt to establish PA sovereignty or to maintain PA autonomy in some parts of the Land of Israel, the idea is innovative in that it, even if only partially, begins to debunk the flawed notion that Israel has to surrender land to have peace and security.

Those on the right of the Israeli political spectrum should avoid the tendency to crown Sisi as Israel's savior. While Sisi is certainly to be applauded for thinking out of the box, he is also acting from at least a little bit of self-interest, as the tenuous, unstable status of a militarized Gaza has been one big headache for him.

However, despite the good intentions, any official peace arrangement with the Hamas-Fatah Unity PA will lead to continued warfare, because their goal remains the destruction of Israel and their promises have proven worthless.

The bottom line: Nothing short of the complete dissolution of the PA and the implementation of full Israeli sovereignty in Judea, Samaria, and Gaza will bring peace and security to Israel.

Facing ISIS Or Facing Hamas:
When A War Is Not A War

"There is no avoiding war; it can only be postponed to the advantage of others."

Niccolo Machiavelli, 15th century Italian historian, writer

US President Barack Obama has now garnered international support for a widespread war operation against the Islamic State (IS or ISIS or ISIL) terrorist organization in Iraq and Syria, but in an interview with CBS News State Department Correspondent Margaret Brennan, his Secretary of State John Kerry seems afraid of calling it a war:

"We're engaged in a major counter-terrorism operation, and it's going to be a long-term counter-terrorism operation. I think war is the wrong terminology and analogy but the fact is that we are engaged in a very significant global effort to curb terrorist activity," Kerry said.

Similarly, throughout its Operation Protective Edge in Gaza, Israel's political leadership refused to call it a war. Does it really matter? Is it all just a meaningless game of semantics?

Well, it is semantics, but it's certainly not meaningless. Just as the Roman conquerors changed the name of the Land of Israel to Palestina after exiling most of its Jews almost 2,000 years ago and just as the Arab nations in 1948 started calling Judea and Samaria by the non-historical term, the West Bank, so, too, with the use of a word like war.

Words matter, but as is frequently the case in public

affairs, it all boils down to politics and economics, which have influenced the semantics used by both Israeli Prime Minister Netanyahu and President Obama. Obama is looking after his political base of far left, radical anti-war extremists, for whom a declaration of war, even against Adolf Hitler, would be considered barbaric, and, of course, imperialistic. Furthermore, Obama can't declare war against an Islamic entity of any kind – even if there are Muslims in his non-war coalition. This is due to his promise, made shortly after his election in 2008, which vowed that the United States "will never be at war with the Islamic world." No doubt this promise was influenced by his Islamic upbringing (yes, I know he says he's a Christian). To this date, Obama firmly adheres to his pledge not to use the word Islamic in the same breath as the word terrorism. Yes, yes, of course, we all know that there is absolutely no connection between terrorism and that great monotheistic religion!

In the case of Netanyahu, a declaration of war against Hamas would have further increased the anger of Obama about the Israeli operation, however justified it was. Netanyahu, being cautious, even hyper-sensitive to world criticism, wouldn't take such a chance. A declaration of war would have also legally required wider economic compensation to those Israelis suffering damages from the fighting. Being a conservative economist, Netanyahu wanted to avoid that at all costs.

There is, however, a very clear reason to declare war, especially when fighting an Islamic terrorist enemy. Declaring war against Islamic terrorist organizations such as Islamic State or Hamas provides a psychological edge to the American or Israeli soldiers who are facing a vicious terrorist enemy that plays by the rules of Jihad, or holy war against "the unbelievers." When we understand that we are indeed playing by the rules of war, in which it's understood that civilians will get hurt, it gives the free world more leverage in defeating an immoral enemy that hides among civilians and knows no respect for human life.

The Islamic Ghost That Haunts Obama

"I will stand with the Muslims should the political winds shift in an ugly direction."

US President Barack Obama

We are all influenced by our backgrounds. With the 2008 election of Barack Obama, who has fundamentally attempted to change America's orientation in the world, thereby impacting Israel in very negative ways, I began to explore my relationship with the USA as one who was born and raised there. I fully identify as an Israeli – I married in Israel, my children were all born in Israel, my message is fundamentally a message of Israel's mission, and my work is totally focused on building Israel's biblical heartland through the children of Israel. Furthermore, when I travel and speak to groups across the United States, Canada, and elsewhere, I am doing so as an Israeli, even though I may have insights into American realities that most Israeli natives probably don't possess.

Nonetheless, I still identify as an American as well, a fact of which I am proud and which I have integrated into my worldview as an Israeli. We are a product of where we come from, in addition to our essence, and in addition to the many influences that we absorb along the way. I am sure that on that sociological point President Obama and I would agree, based as well on his experience living briefly in Hawaii and/ or Kenya, and Indonesia and growing up as a (possibly non-practicing) Muslim – or at least being registered as a Muslim attending school in Indonesia before moving to America and later undergoing an interesting religious transformation in a particularly controversial church.

Whether Barack Hussein Obama identifies as a Muslim or as a Christian (which he claims to), the fact is that he had a Muslim father (which according to Islam makes one a Muslim) and then a Muslim step-father. Obama idolized his father, as we saw in his autobiographical book, "Dreams From My Father" and perhaps for that reason, he has seemed to be in perpetual awe of Islam, as we have seen in his public references to "the holy Koran," as opposed to his almost mocking references to the Torah, or the Bible of Israel.

Having said all that, the key problem with the influence of Obama's background is that he is the POTUS, the leader of a free world that is being assaulted by an Islamic monster that has been seriously threatening Israel, America, and Western civilization for years. Those threats have been noticeably heightened with the rise of the Islamic State (ISIS or ISIL or IS) terrorist organization that has been terrorizing minorities in the Middle East and has been beheading American and British citizens.

Despite his awesome responsibility as president, and despite the demands of the moment, Obama seems unable to transcend his background in the religion of "Jihad," or holy war against the unbelievers. He continues his ongoing nonsensical mantra that Islam is not dangerous, that Islam is not a basis for terrorism, that Islam is a progressive religion.

According to Obama:

> *"Now let's make two things clear: ISIL is not 'Islamic.'*
> *No religion condones the killing of innocents."*

Sadly, that could not be farther from the truth. The classic Islamic sources have revealed to us that Muhammad, the founder of Islam, who all Muslims revere and follow, beheaded between 600-900 Jews in one day. Would Obama dare say that those many hundreds of Jewish victims of Muhammad's wrath weren't innocent?

Furthermore, Islamic sources reveal that the beatings and rapes of young women and the sexual abuse of children that are now being widely carried out, not just by, but especially by ISIS, are simply an extreme manifestation of the teachings and actions of Muhammad, who tolerated, advocated, and/ or carried out sexual abuse and beatings of women.

The bottom line? There is nothing more Islamic than ISIS, which carries out the Jihadist, abusive ideology that is at the core of Islam. What is truly absurd is that an apologist for Islam is the ostensible leader of the free world's struggle against Islam's most assertive manifestation. Sadly, Obama's Islamic biases will continue to get in the way.

Can Religious Zionists Lead Israel?

"If there is no sovereignty – There is no Zionism."

Naftali Bennett, Israeli Cabinet Minister,
Chairman of Jewish Home Party

The controversy over Jewish Home party leader Naftali Bennett's internal power grab has raised several nagging questions about the resurgent Religious Zionist movement. Those who care about that movement's political success should be concerned, but not necessarily for the reasons that have been fiercely debated in several media forums.

The main questions can be broken down as follows:

1. Is Bennett abandoning the values of Religious Zionism by opening up the Jewish Home party to Russian Jews and Druze?

2. Is Bennett's desire to be prime minister more important to him than the ideological purity of the movement?

3. Is Bennett seeking to turn the party into another Likud?

Whether one agrees with the harshness of the criticism or not, these are legitimate questions that should be discussed, but the need for unity should be central in any dialogue. While there are certain individuals for whom national-religious unity is less important than ideological purity, most Religious Zionists would agree that there will always be a spectrum of opinions within the movement, and that sitting helplessly with 2-5 seats in the wilderness of the opposition is not a position that we want to go back to.

Naftali Bennett has proven to be a remarkable politician, with an ability to bring people together, and that has led to the rejuvenated Jewish Home party's relative success with its 12 seats in the Knesset. The desire to expand further to attract many of the mostly secular/traditional/nationalistic Russian Jews and Druze voters is a positive step that can greatly increase the leverage of the party in the formation of the next government. In all of the recent debate, there has been little convincing evidence presented to buttress the charge that enabling greater inclusion will lead to the abandonment of Religious Zionist values. The precedent of the very popular MK Ayelet Shaked is a case in point. While considered secular in her personal observance, Shaked has proven herself to be very respectful of religious values, has acted consistent to the party platform in her legislative activity, and has remained faithful to her previous reputation as an outspoken nationalist. That precedent should be a guideline for any "secular," or less traditional candidates that may be brought in as potential members of the next Jewish Home list. It should be pointed out that in the last election, the only party considered to be to the right of Jewish Home also did not have a list consisting just of religious purists. There will always be debate and differences of opinion in any party and that is legitimate, as long as the overall party platform is adhered to.

As for the strategy of reaching out to those who would not have been Jewish Home members in the past, this should have been done years ago to increase the rather stagnant voter base of the Mafdal (the old National Religious Party and all of its periodic offshoots with their rather pathetic 2-3 seat Knesset factions). While Shas was rapidly expanding its voter base despite its non-Zionistic positions, and while the Likud was attracting national-religious voters despite its anti-national religious election campaigns, the Mafdal/ Jewish Home never really expanded its potential voter base to include those who want to see a more traditional and more Zionistic Israel, even if their personal observance is less traditional. Bennett's change of direction in aggressively pursuing those voters, which parties like Shas have done for years, spurred the Jewish Home's remarkable growth in the last election, and its continued growth in the polls since then. In fact, Shas has always appealed for votes from less religious voters, but has always remained faithful to its principles and has continued to consult its rabbis. There is no reason why Jewish Home can't do the same, and, as a strongly Zionistic party, can do it much better, even with a few "out-of-the-box" candidates.

There has long been great frustration on the Right about Prime Minister Netanyahu's refusal to allow the sorely needed building of homes in the liberated areas of Judea and Samaria, a state of affairs that has not improved much since the last election, even though Jewish Home MK Uri Ariel is Housing Minister. And that is the proof that despite the recent growth, being merely the third largest party in the coalition is not enough. Like it or not, it is the prime minister who determines the direction of national policy on issues such as building policy in Judea, Samaria, and eastern Jerusalem and it's not likely to change as long as the Netanyahu-led Likud and the left-of-center Yesh Atid are overwhelmingly the two largest parties.

The real question is not whether Naftali Bennett wants to be prime minister, but whether Religious Zionists want to greatly increase their power in the fulfillment of critical goals such as strengthening national-religious education, protecting the complete Land of Israel, and asserting Jewish sovereignty. Only a large and powerful Jewish Home, with at least 18-20 seats in the Knesset, can truly make that happen. If the current party platform remains the same, with all candidates promising to be faithful to that platform, and if Bennett continues to seek rabbinical guidance about the overall direction of the party, then the recent panic about the perceived shift in political strategy is greatly exaggerated.

Haredi Leaders
And The Dangerous Use Of Words

"Why was the second Temple destroyed? Because of Sinat Chinam, senseless hatred of one Jew for another."

Talmud

At which point do differences of opinion on critical national issues become a verbal vendetta of unethical name-calling used to slander those who disagree with you?

After Minister Gideon Saar's recently announced retirement from politics, MK Yisrael Eichler of the United Torah Judaism party crossed the line once again with his public comments, exploiting the resignation to refer to Israel's current government as an "evil government." Despite the attention-grabbing statements of media-savvy politicians like Eichler, such slurs are usually not responded to. This is mainly due to the reluctance of the targets of such attacks to create further conflict by stirring the boiling pot. However, there is a serious problem with the loose use of such harsh labeling by leading Haredi (ultra-Orthodox) politicians or rabbis, and it needs to be addressed.

In his dangerous use of words, MK Eichler joins his Knesset colleague, Uri Maklev, who several months ago referred to the current coalition as a "government of destruction, evil and annihilation," inflammatory words that are usually saved for Nebuchadnezzar, the Romans, or the worst of the Czars, but not for one's fellow Jews. In addition, we have seen the Sinat Chinam (needless hatred) of Rabbi Shalom Cohen, the head of the reconstituted Shas Council of Torah Sages, who has fiercely attacked the Religious Zionist population on several occasions, calling its members "Amalek," among other slurs, thus comparing national-religious Jews to the biblical enemy of Israel that we are all commanded to totally obliterate.

Presumably, the harsh terminology towards other Jews stems from the Haredi anger about the new, somewhat more equitable, draft system, which broadens the draft to include young Haredim, as well as encouraging them to join the tax-paying work force, as well. One can perhaps understand the Haredi establishment's concern that many of the youth will become soldiers, thereby threatening their long-standing dependence on the yeshiva system from which they indirectly receive social welfare benefits, often well into their adult years. There are, indeed, a lot of people who have a financial stake in that system.

If the fear that Torah learning in Israel will be reduced is truly the main concern, these Haredi spokesmen/leaders would do well to find ways to use their knowledge of Torah to increase Torah learning among other segments of the population that haven't had the privilege of delving into and reaping the wisdom of the Jewish sources. After all, the Torah was given to all of Israel, not just to one segment of the population, and the prized value of Jewish unity would be well served by not just spreading the obligatory national service, but also by spreading the wisdom of Torah.

During Operation Protective Edge, tens of thousands of Israeli reservists were called to the front in Gaza. Many of them lost their lives in the fighting, while many others were wounded in defense of the nation. Those soldiers were protecting the freedom of every Israeli not just to work and to play, but to learn Torah, as well. Many of these soldiers were Religious Zionists who routinely combine military service with Torah learning, while some of the soldiers were Haredim, and many others were secular or moderately traditional Jews. All were fulfilling the commandment of taking part in a "milchemet mitzvah," an obligatory war, in which all Jews are commanded to leave their study halls and even newly-married young men are commanded to go out and fight for the people of Israel and the Land of Israel, according to the instructions of the God of Israel.

There can be reasonable disagreement about the details of Israel's recent draft law, as there can be about how best to increase Torah learning among Israel's citizens, but there is no excuse that justifies comparing other Jews to the worst of Israel's enemies. We have seen the internal division and the destruction that such words can bring. Yes to dialogue and yes to cooperation, but Eichler and his colleagues should think carefully before spitting out words that will only increase destructive hatred and division in our people.

The Israeli Response
To Mahmoud Abbas's Political "Bomb"

"You punch me, I punch back. I do not believe it's good for one's self-respect to be a punching bag."

Edward Koch, former Mayor of New York City

It has now been confirmed that Palestinian Authority (PA) President Mahmoud Abbas is planning to ask the UN to set a timetable for the end of the Israeli "occupation" and the establishment of a Palestinian state along the pre-1967 borders, with its capital in eastern Jerusalem.

Interviewed in the Palestinian media, top PA official Jibril Rajoub has reported that Abbas will "drop a bomb" on Israel at the UN, presenting his aggressive proposal as part of a "day after" plan following the end of the most recent war in the Gaza Strip.

According to the Qatari News Agency, an agreement to that effect was reached in Abbas's meeting with Qatari Emir Tamim bin Hamad al-Thani and Hamas's political chief Khaled Mashal, in Doha last week.

Despite the fact that such a move by the Hamas-Fatah unity government at the UN is a clear violation of the Oslo Accords, which was the legal basis for the establishment of the Palestinian Authority, Israel's political leadership is eerily silent. One might have thought that after past Israeli warnings to Abbas not to form a unity government with Hamas and not to ignore the Oslo Accords by taking hostile political steps at the UN, we would see Israeli firm action in response to this latest "timetable threat."

The deafening silence from Israeli leaders, who still refer to Mahmoud Abbas affectionately as "Abu Mazen" (Mazen's father), thereby putting a gentle, human face on a deceitful enemy who has continued the PA tradition of directly rewarding terrorists and their families after each terrorist attack, is very disturbing. Despite the blatantly hostile moves taken by Abbas, there have been only weak, temporary responses, and so far, there has been no response to this latest threat, which this time he seems intent on carrying out in honor of Rosh Hashanah, the Jewish New Year. Somehow, the flaccid responses or non-responses from Jerusalem haven't proven to be a convincing deterrent to Abbas's political aggression.

The Israeli response doesn't have to be complicated, but it should be very clearly stated as follows, as a direct response to hostile actions:

1. Once Abbas issues his "timetable" demand at the UN this week, make it clear to him and do so publicly, that the Israeli time clock has started ticking, leading to the dissolution of his Palestinian Authority.

2. The PA was established as a result of an agreement with Israel. Once the PA unilaterally throws the responsibility for making peace over to the UN, that agreement is null and void.

3. The Levy Report, which in 2012 reaffirmed Israel's national rights over Judea and Samaria (the so-called West Bank), should be immediately adopted, thereby replacing the Oslo Accords as the legal basis for government policy in these areas, in which the PA currently has seven autonomous cities and many de facto autonomous towns.

4. The PA should thus be declared "a hostile entity on Israeli soil," with the ramifications of that statement for follow-up Israeli actions to be debated in the Cabinet.

While much was written during Operation Protective Edge about the need to restore Israel's military deterrence, the real problem all along has been our lack of a political deterrence, which causes the world not to take seriously our occasional threats to respond to political aggression.

> *"You make of us an object of strife unto our neighbors, and our enemies laugh amongst themselves."*
>
> Psalms 80:7

Until we start responding with more than empty words to Abbas's long list of hostile actions, Israel's political deterrence will continue to be the laughing stock of the Middle East.

The IDF And The "G" Word

"Be strong and courageous. Do not fear and do not lose resolve, for the Lord your God is with you wherever you will go."

Joshua 1:9

In an interview yesterday with Galei Yisrael (Israel Radio), Defense Minister Moshe Yaalon sharply criticized Givati Brigade Commander Col. Ofer Winter for religious statements he had made to his soldiers during Operation Protective Edge.

What did Col. Winter actually say that inspired this rebuke? Let's examine his words, as well as the response of Minister Yaalon:

Winter:
"We have planned and prepared for this moment and we take the mission upon ourselves out of commitment, complete humility, and because we are prepared to endanger ourselves and lay down our lives in order to protect our families, our people and our homeland."

Winter then invoked the Shema – the traditional Jewish prayer of allegiance to the one God – and called upon "the God of Israel" to "make our path successful as we go and stand to fight for the sake of Your people of Israel against a foe which curses Your name."

Yaalon:
"There are also Druze, and Bedouin, and Christian

Arabs and Muslim Arabs, and therefore when we speak as commanders, we need to speak to all and not just to a particular segment ... In that I think commanders should carefully guard the IDF as the Israel Defense Forces (IDF) and not the Defense Forces of a particular group."

So who is right? Is it wrong to talk about God to Israel's soldiers?

Prime Minister Binyamin Netanyahu has often insisted that Israel be recognized as the "nation-state" of the Jewish people. There is no nation-state in the world that has a stronger tradition of connection to God than Israel. To ignore this connection, to prevent any references to God, would be contrary to who we are as a people.

The objections come mainly from those who don't believe in a Higher Power. Certainly there are atheists among us, but according to recent polls, they are a rapidly shrinking minority, with well over 80% of Israeli Jews clearly expressing belief in God. Even some of the kibbutzim of the previously anti-religious HaShomer Ha'tzair movement have organized traditional religious services for Rosh Hashanah in recent years, and they are growing in numbers.

As the Jamaican Reggae singer Bob Marley was wont to say, "A person without knowledge of his heritage is like a tree without roots." And a thirsty tree, I might add, is one that seeks to nourish those roots.

Whether individual Jews fully observe the commandments as described in the Torah is not the issue. The Balfour Declaration and League of Nations approval notwithstanding, our claim as Jews to the Land of Israel is ultimately based on our connection to the Almighty as delineated in the Torah. To ignore and even forbid the expression of that heritage is to tie the hands of our soldiers. The heritage of Israel is indeed our raison d'etre, a very firm justification for our existence here in our country. If our soldiers are "the Israel Defense Forces," as Yaalon pointed out, then it is indeed the heritage of Israel that will give us the strength to meet the multiple challenges that we are facing in a hostile world.

As for the minorities living in Israel, it is likely that among them, a large majority believe in God, with Christians and Druze certainly believing in the God of Israel, otherwise known as the God of Abraham, Isaac, and Jacob. As for Muslims, only a very small number serve in the IDF, and most of them say that they believe in God. However, if they do, it better be the God of Israel, not the Allah of Islam's Koran and Hadith, which says to chop off the fingertips of the "unbelievers" and boasts about the beheadings and the murder of Jews and "infidels."

Then again, we'll leave that topic for a separate article.

Wishing the Israel Defense Forces much success in its future battles – with God's help, of course!

Stop Apologizing And Start Building!

"For the people shall dwell in Zion at Jerusalem; you shall weep no more."

Isaiah 30:19

When does an ally cease to be an ally? This painful question is being asked by many Israelis after another blistering American attack on Israel's sovereignty in its capital city, Jerusalem.

In a move certain to increase tensions between Israel and the United States, White House Press Secretary Josh Earnest publicly criticized Israel for allowing the continuation of the planning process for homes in the Givat Hamatos area in south Jerusalem. Not skipping a beat, State Department Spokeswoman Jen Psaki followed suit and sharpened the dagger, saying "This development will only draw condemnation from the international community, distance Israel from even its closest allies, poison the atmosphere not only with the Palestinians but also with the very Arab governments with which Prime Minister Netanyahu said he wanted to build relations."

This very public American disrespect of a reliable ally's sovereignty is shocking, and it should be condemned by Israeli officials in the strongest language. There is absolutely no reason why Israeli officials should feel the need, as they apparently did, to justify their actions with apologetic statements about how the Givat Hamatos project was just a "technical step" taken at the local level on a plan approved at the regional level over two years ago. Instead, Prime Minister

Binyamin (Bibi) Netanyahu should immediately cease being apologetic and defensive in responding to this recurring, blatant assault on Israel's sovereignty. Yes, Bibi was correct to complain about the implication by American officials that Israel should discriminate against Jews, but he should also respond forcefully that if President Barack Obama was a true friend of Israel, he wouldn't criticize the granting of building permits for homes for Israeli citizens in Israel's capital city, Jerusalem. Would Obama dare to criticize building approvals in Riyadh, in Amman, or in Cairo? This needs to be stated and stated clearly.

However, words are not enough. Binyamin Netanyahu has always been a powerful speaker, but the reality on the ground usually contradicts his words. Netanyahu has, in fact, been one of the least proactive prime ministers when it comes to advancing building projects in Jerusalem. Notwithstanding his bold statements about Israel's eternal capital, where the prophets spoke and where kings of Israel such as David and Solomon ruled 3,000 years ago, and which Israel liberated in the Six Day War of 1967, Bibi has been pathetically weak in asserting Israel's rights in its capital city. Sadly, the lack of action speaks louder than the impressive words. The always spoken about, but never advanced, E-1 building project in the large forsaken area between Jerusalem's French Hill neighborhood and the city of Maale Adumim to its east, is a glaring example of that weakness under pressure.

It's time to stop complaining about American statements and to start acting. One doesn't have to go back too far in history to see how prime ministers such as Menachem Begin and Yitzhak Shamir ignored international pressure and aggressively advanced the building of whole neighborhoods like Pisgat Ze'ev and Givat Ze'ev in the liberated areas of eastern and northern Jerusalem. We Israelis have nothing to apologize for and a lot to be proud of. Let's start being faithful to our statements about our deep roots in this land. Let's take real action to advance the building process in our capital city. E-1 would be a very good start.

Be Fruitful, Multiply …
And Protect Those Borders

"And God blessed them, and God said unto them, Be fruitful, and multiply; and replenish the earth …"

Genesis 1:28

B eing such a tiny country, we in Israel often forget that we have a lot to teach the world, but teach doesn't mean preach. It's usually just a matter of setting a good example.

Contrary to the mainstream of Western civilization, Israel continues to buck the problematic trends on the international demographic front. And that's good news.

The average non-Muslim American family has approximately two children per family, if that many, and of course a dog and a cat (Note the increase in the number of "pet department stores" in American cities as opposed to baby stores). More troubling than that negative statistic is the fact that the average Muslim family has far more, usually in the range of five or six children per family. On the European continent, the rates are even more shocking, with the average non-Muslim family having far less than two children per family, while Muslim families are having several times more. All one has to do is some simple arithmetic to see where it's going. As Western civilization moves further and further away from traditional child-centered families, it is gradually self-destructing before our very eyes. Even more disturbing is that most Europeans and Americans seem either unaware or helpless in combating this ominous trend, despite the fact that there are many solutions, most of which I describe in my book, "The Islamic Tsunami: Israel and America in the Age of Obama."

The glimmer of brightness in the darkness is that Israel is becoming a demographic light unto the nations. According to the latest demographic research reported by the Central Bureau of Statistics, the birth rate of Israeli Muslims is continuing to fall, as the Jewish birthrate rises. In 2013, the average Muslim family in Israel had 3.4 children, a significant fall from the 4.7 children recorded in 2000. While the Muslim birthrate is still higher than the rising Jewish rate, which now stands at 3.1, the gap is rapidly closing, and all indications are that the Jewish rate will surpass that of the Muslims in the next few years.

Let's be encouraged by these positive trends, which significantly, are being seen across the Jewish political/ religious spectrum, although the largest families and the fastest growth rates are still being felt in the biblical heartland of Judea, Samaria, and Jerusalem.

Coupled with all of this good birth news are the ongoing reports of sharply reduced illegal immigration into Israel, the result of strong action taken by the Israeli government to protect Israel's borders from illegal infiltration. Could it be that our friends in North America have what to learn from us?

An Open Letter To "J Street"

"Serious misfortunes, originating in misrepresentation, frequently flow and spread before they can be dissipated by truth."

George Washington, American President

D ear Jeremy Ben-Ami and the ostensibly "pro-Israel" J Street,
After your latest outburst, slamming Prime Minister Binyamin Netanyahu's defense of the Givat Hamatos building project in Jerusalem, I feel compelled to respond, from the personal perspective of one who lives in Israel.

I am a proud resident of the reestablished ancient city of Shiloh in Samaria, the region that you mistakenly call "the Israeli-occupied West Bank." My mother lives in our liberated capital of Jerusalem, which the Obama administration that you firmly support, refers to as "Israeli-occupied East Jerusalem." And yes, I know that you have referred to the building of neighborhoods in our capital city as "illegal settlements," not to mention your ignorant criticism of the revival of Jewish life in Judea and Samaria, our biblical heartland, liberated by Israel in the 1967 Six Day War.

If it were just a matter of semantics, I could perhaps consider you to be merely ignorant of history. I could explain to you that Samuel the Prophet grew up in Shiloh, during the 369 years that Shiloh was Israel's capital, far longer than the age of your country, the USA. I could also explain to you that the great Kings of Israel, David and Solomon, reigned in the Old (eastern) City of Jerusalem, and that Israel was sovereign there for many hundreds of years, also much longer than the age of the United States. Did you know that the Jewish people in exile, your people, for nearly 2,000 years have prayed in the direction of the Temple Mount in eastern Jerusalem, where the holy Temple twice stood, before being destroyed by Israel's enemies?

Furthermore, are you aware that the Arab nations, after failing to drive the Jews into the sea from 1948 to 1964, adopted a new political strategy whereby they would create a new underdog, calling the mostly Muslim residents of the Land of Israel by the fictional term "Palestinians," thus adopting that old Roman misnomer as their own?

The fact is that there never was a country called Palestine here. If you doubt that, I challenge you to answer this very simple question: What was the monetary currency of that ancient nation that you claim we are occupying?

While there are some peoples, such as the Kurds, that perhaps deserve their own country, there is absolutely no historical nor social justification for the creation of such a nation of Palestine, which, if allowed to be born under its current Fatah-Hamas leadership, would undoubtedly become another legitimized Islamic terrorist stronghold.

If it was only a question of clearing up your ignorance of history, we could sit and review the facts, but your recent remarks go way beyond historical ignorance and enter the realm of political deception.

For instance:

"Palestinians are not allowed ... to drive on Israeli-only roads connecting these settlements through 'security zones' surrounding the settlements."

This is an absolute falsehood. Everyone who lives in Jerusalem knows that the Arabs roam freely through the streets of Jerusalem, while Jews are often violently attacked if they dare to enter the Arab neighborhoods.

As for Samaria and Judea (your so-called West Bank), a Jew doesn't dare to drive with his car window open for fear of rock or firebomb attack, whereas Arabs almost always drive with windows open.

I cannot enter the Arab city of Ramallah for fear of death, but Arabs drive freely on Route 60 (the Road of the Patriarchs), which connects the Jewish communities of Samaria.

Perhaps a visit to Israel, including its liberated capital and heartland, would be an eye-opening experience for you. It's certainly easier to live one's life in an intellectual cocoon, but there is a lot of real learning that can be done outside of your comfort zone of Washington, DC amongst the Obama administration's untruths about Israel and the Middle East. Are you prepared to crawl out of that box? Are you ready to meet the challenge?

America Praises
And Supports Terrorist Government

"I will bless those who bless you, and him who curses you I will curse; and all nations on the earth will be blessed through you."

Genesis 12:3

The post-Gaza war period has seen some disturbing statements and actions by the United States political leadership that call into serious question its reliability, as the leader of the free world and as a trusted ally of Israel.

The American air attacks on the Islamic State (otherwise known as ISIS, ISIL or IS) savages in support of the relatively pro-Western Kurds and other minorities in Iraq are positive, if somewhat insufficient, and are continuing, but contradictory and conspicuous lack of action against ISIS has been revealed in Syria. On that front, the Americans have been reluctant to offend President Obama's close confidant Prime Minister Recep Tayyip Erdogan of Turkey, whose repressive anti-Kurd (not to mention anti-Israel) policies are well known.

Closer to home, the latest evidence that Uncle Sam can no longer be counted on is its reaction to the first meeting of the Palestinian Authority (PA) unity government in Gaza. The Hamas-Fatah leadership meeting was praised by US State Department Spokesperson Jen Psaki as "a positive step." So that we won't doubt that its words will also be followed by actions, the Obama administration has already pledged approximately $330 million to rebuild Gaza since Hamas's latest terror war on Israel. The stated rationale is that the money won't go to Hamas, but will instead go through the PA "government of technocrats."

Lest we naively assume that America's political leadership truly believes this malarkey, it should be pointed out that a little déjà vu can be learned from:

RAMALLAH, December 7, 2006 (WAFA) – President Mahmoud Abbas said Thursday that "our goal to end the current crisis is to form a national technocrat government whose concern would be ending the siege imposed on the Palestinian people."

Been there, done that, and hopefully, we Israelis won't be fooled again. In the succeeding seven plus years, Abbas's "government of technocrats" has efficiently handed out hundreds of millions of dollars to the terrorists and their families, with a technocratic efficiency that would have made Adolf Eichmann proud. And mind you, Mahmoud Abbas is an equal opportunity employer – his funds are efficiently disbursed by his technocrats, not just to Fatah terrorists, but also to terrorists from Hamas, Islamic Jihad, and any other terrorist organization that is active in the PA autonomous territories.

Whether the Americans believe that the Hamas-Fatah terrorist authority can be trusted is not the question that we need to be asking. The answer to that question should by now be quite obvious. The more troubling question that nobody wants to ask is whether we can trust the Americans. Yes, the Iron Dome defensive system, partially funded by the United States, has saved many lives and for that we are grateful to the Americans for their financial support. However, when it comes to actual policy, Obama has not been on Israel's side, and has in fact stood with Israel's bitter enemies.

If Israel were to suddenly announce its support for ISIS,

Americans would certainly, and correctly, feel betrayed. Similarly, the consistent American support for Israel's enemies Hamas, Fatah, and Islamic Jihad is an ongoing act of betrayal of a loyal ally, and we shouldn't pretend otherwise.

It will cause some friction and will perhaps, inadvertently, hurt the chances of some Democrats in the mid-term elections, but such a betrayal of a loyal American ally should be emphasized and denounced publicly.

The Gaza Rehab: Lessons Not Learned

"Who is wise and will understand these things; who is understanding and will know them?"

Hosea 14:10

A t the conclusion of the recent donors' conference for Gaza, which Norway co-hosted, Foreign Minister Boerge Brende proudly announced, "The participants pledged approximately $5.4 billion (4.3 billion euros)." Half of the pledges will go for Gaza reconstruction and the rest as unspecified aid to the Palestinians, he said.

The stated goal of the conference is to finance the reconstruction of parts of the Gaza region that were destroyed in the July-August war between Israel and Hamas. Meanwhile, Israeli Foreign Minister Avigdor Liberman warned that no financial aid will be sent to Gaza without Israel's approval. Any concerned observer has to wonder who to believe and whose words to trust.

Now that we have reached this post-war stage, in which the Palestinian Authority (PA) Hamas-Fatah unity government is trying to reap the political/financial rewards of the most recent conflict, it would be wise for Israel to learn the lessons, lest the terrorists collect the dividends.

Although many Israelis disagree, one can reasonably assert that the Gaza war was a military victory for Israel, but it certainly was a political-strategic loss. The primary demand made by Israel at the end of the fighting was that Gaza be demilitarized as a condition for rehabilitation. This has not happened, nor does it appear that it will happen. No mention was made of demilitarization at the recent conference and Hamas has reaffirmed over and over again that not one gun will be taken away from its fighters. Meanwhile, Israel's Prime Minister Binyamin Netanyahu has been conspicuously silent about his formerly iron-clad condition of demilitarization.

Furthermore, rumors are rampant about an impending prisoner swap between Israel and Hamas that will include the release of hundreds of living Hamas terrorist prisoners, in exchange for the bodies of the two dead Israeli soldiers. If history repeats itself, which it usually does, those released terrorists will soon be active again, as we saw with the terrorists released in the infamous Gilad Shalit deal, most of whom quickly returned to terrorist activity, and many of whom were rearrested during the Gaza fighting. It should be obvious that if they are released again, they will speedily return to their professional terrorist activity, which is heavily funded by the PA.

Meanwhile, Netanyahu will make some empty, but impressive-sounding threats on American television and Liberman will make some vacuous statements about how his word is his word, but after some quiet negotiation and American assurances of the PA's peaceful intentions, all threats will be forgotten.

At least a portion of the promised billions will flow into Gaza, and at least a portion of those funds will go towards renewed terrorist infrastructure and the purchase or manufacture of new weaponry. Simultaneously, the released terrorists will quietly "go back to work," with terrorist salaries paid by the PA, and Defense Minister Yaalon will promise to "hit them hard" and to "respond forcefully" if the rockets start falling again.

Am I perhaps being overly cynical? I honestly wish that were so, but the lessons of past ceasefires and "peace plans" tell us otherwise. Unless Israel's flawed behavior patterns of the past are corrected, history will repeat itself.

Revoking Israeli Citizenship? Why Just ISIS Members?

(Hamas is) "not a violent religious group."

Hamas Leader Khaled Mashal

Tourism Minister Uzi Landau has written a letter to Prime Minister Binyamin Netanyahu, requesting that he revoke the citizenship of Israelis enlisting in the Islamic State (otherwise known as ISIS or ISIL or IS) terrorist organization.

ISIS, which is increasingly terrorizing countless communities throughout the Middle East, with sights unabashedly aimed around the world, has been actively recruiting Arab Israelis to join its ranks. Israeli security services are reporting that over thirty Israeli citizens have enrolled to date.

Landau wrote:

> *"These are people who live in Israel as citizens, and as such they enjoy a long list of rights, as well as access to large and sensitive information ... It is just a question of time until these people, living among us, become a lethal weapon directed against us."*

While one can certainly agree wholeheartedly with Minister Landau's request, it should be pointed out that the problem isn't only ISIS. There are far more Arab Israelis who are members of Hamas and of Islamic Jihad. Shouldn't their citizenship be revoked, as well?

Yes, there are some notable differences in strategy. ISIS is more "in your face" than the others, but they all share the same ideology of Jihad, or holy war against all non-Muslims. This ideology is manifested in the Sunni Muslim doctrine of the Muslim Brotherhood, and is firmly rooted in the teachings of the founder of Islam, Muhammad. Why not revoke the citizenship and expel (or not allow the return of) all Arab Israelis who join these Islamic terrorist organizations? Israeli security concerns shouldn't be based on misguided foreign (American or European Union) tolerance for non-ISIS terrorist organizations. Israeli citizenship is a privilege, and Israeli citizens who wish to destroy their own country and are enrolling in ISIS, Hamas, or Islamic Jihad should have that privilege removed.

Other countries are also suffering from this phenomenon and with them, as well, the problem extends beyond ISIS. Nonetheless, we cannot wait for others to act. Israel must lead on this issue, acting decisively to carve out the growing cancer in its midst.

In Retrospect: The Latest Kerry Fiasco

"Beware of false knowledge; it is more dangerous than ignorance."

George Bernard Shaw, Irish playwright

Israel's Defense Minister Moshe Yaalon (Likud) was quite upset at Economy Minister Naftali Bennett (Jewish Home) for his very public criticism of US Secretary of State John Kerry. While it is understandable that such criticism puts Yaalon in a slightly uncomfortable position on the eve of his upcoming meetings in Washington, it must be said that Kerry has, indeed, revealed an uncanny ignorance of the Middle East with his latest statements, which certainly seemed to imply that Israel is to blame for the rise of ISIS and other manifestations of Islamic extremism in the region. Such comments, definitely intended for public consumption, should not go unanswered, so therefore, let's examine his words in retrospect.

Said Kerry:

> *"There wasn't a leader I met with in the region who didn't raise with me spontaneously the need to try to get peace between Israel and the Palestinians, because it was a cause of recruitment and of street anger and agitation ... People need to understand the connection of that. And it has something to do with humiliation and denial and absence of dignity."*

Which leaders was he speaking about? Who are those moral leaders whose advice he trusts? Could it be Recep Tayyip Erdogan of Turkey – who has refused to put troops on the ground to fight ISIS and has done his utmost to torpedo American efforts to assist the Kurds, who are under fierce attack by ISIS? Or could Kerry be talking about King Abdullah of Saudi Arabia – whose female citizens aren't allowed to drive and whose husbands are legally allowed to physically abuse them? Or perhaps Kerry was referring to a moral authority such as Mahmoud Abbas – whose Palestinian Authority pays salaries to Hamas, Fatah, and Islamic Jihad terrorists who have proudly slaughtered and maimed thousands of Israeli children?

Whether knowingly or not, Kerry continues to parrot the false, but by now well-known, "new underdog" narrative of the Islamic world, in which Israel, and only Israel, is blamed for denying the "rights" of the "Palestinians," while raising that defamation to new levels by strangely implying that such "denial of rights" has caused the rise of ISIS.

True, Yaalon was angry at Bennett for his public criticism of Kerry, which set the stage for a possible tongue-lashing from the White House upon Yaalon's arrival in Washington. However, there comes a time when we need to stop tip-toeing around the issues, so as not to "offend" the big master in DC, for fear of losing financial assistance, which won't be cut off anyhow. It's instructive to remember that American military aid may be good for Israel, but the United States stands with Israel primarily because it's in America's interests, and for that reason, there is support for Israel across the aisle in Congress (even if it is stronger these days on the Republican side).

In any event, Kerry's apparent ignorance of Middle East realities revealed by his misuse of terms like "humiliation," "denial," and "absence of dignity" is troubling and shows a disturbing lack of understanding of the facts, and it is this misunderstanding of these loaded terms that needs to be explained to him:

1. "Humiliation" is what the Islamic terrorists around the world are trying to do to the rest of us with their violent attacks on all those who disagree with them, attacks that are expressed both physically and verbally.

2. "Denial" is the religious/culture war that they are carrying out against free people throughout Western civilization, in which Islamic terrorists are forcing people to live in fear of speaking the truth about the goal of Islamic domination that is inherent in Islamic theology (Jihad – holy war against non-Muslims). People are being repeatedly told by the head honcho in the White House that it is forbidden to even mouth the expression "Islamic Terrorism."

3. "Absence of dignity", last but not least, is the inability of Israeli children to walk and play in certain parts of their country, without fear that Islamic terrorists will murder them with weapons provided by the 5.4 billion in funds that were raised for Hamas, with the help of none other than John Kerry.

John Kerry should apologize to every Israeli and every American fighting ISIS and other Islamic terrorists for his erroneous comments, which are far removed from the reality here in the Middle East. If he truly wanted to learn the facts, he would do what Thomas Jefferson did when confronted with the Islamic terrorism of the Barbary Pirates – to get a copy of the Koran, in order to learn about the Islamic mentality and the growing popularity of its Jihadist ideology, which are the real cause for the rise of Islamic extremism.

If reading the Koran is a bit overwhelming for him, he can always get a copy of my book, "The Islamic Tsunami: Israel and America in the Age of Obama." He might learn a few things about Israel, Islamic terrorism, the Middle East, and how all of this relates to ISIS and the beheading of Americans.

Rejoicing In Children, Rejoicing In Life

"And the streets of the city will be filled (once again) with boys and girls playing in its streets."

Zechariah 8:5

After today's horrific terrorist attack in Jerusalem, Hamas spokesman Hossam Badran announced on official Hamas television:

"This is a natural response to the crimes of the occupation and invasion of our land by the Jews ..."

Such an obscene statement by a sick Islamic extremist, with absolutely no basis in historical fact, is usually not worthy of a response. However, after his rejoicing in the brutal terrorist murder of a three-month-old baby in Jerusalem, and the wounding of eight other Israelis today, the question must again be asked – What kinds of savages would justify and glorify the murder of innocent children?

We have experienced this many times before: I immediately think of a former Shiloh resident, five-month-old Yehudah Shoham, critically wounded when terrorists threw a giant rock at his head, as he was sitting in the baby seat with his parents in their car. He died from his wounds a few days later.

Another sad story is the death of ten-month-old Hebron resident Shalhevet Pass, murdered by an Arab sniper that was clearly aiming to kill her.

Then, of course, there is the horrible story of the Fogel

family in Itamar, in which more than half the family, including both parents and several of their young children, were murdered in cold blood in their home by terrorist infiltrators.

These painful stories have been repeated too many times and have torn apart far too many families, but the terrorists, who derive the justification for their acts from the sick, Jihadist philosophy that is central in Islam, know no remorse – for Jihad – which in practice means holy war against non-Muslims, rejoices in the death of innocent children.

We Israelis, as most people in Western civilization, find such a mentality shocking. Sometime after my then three-year-old son and I were wounded in a terrorist shooting attack (and miraculously survived), I founded the Shiloh Israel Children's Fund (SICF) to heal the trauma of the terror victim children and to rebuild the biblical heartland of Israel through those children. Aside from our main therapeutic and educational projects, SICF sponsors camps for children, where the children learn to swim, to play sports, to play music, and to hike. When Hamas sponsors camps for children, the children are taught to fire rifles at "the Jews and infidels" and to die for "Allah."

It's critical for our survival as the nation of Israel, and for the survival of the free world, to remember that we are being confronted with an enemy that has a very different mentality than ours. While we rejoice in our children's lives, they rejoice in their deaths, and even in the deaths of their own.

We will not be discouraged by their hatred, nor by their love of murder and death. We will not cease to confront them on the front lines of the war on Islamic terrorism and I will continue to call on our political leadership to take forceful action. With God's help, I have no doubt that despite all of our pain, we will triumph. We will continue to rejoice in life and to build for the future through the children.

Some US Citizens
Are More Equal Than Others

"All animals are equal, but some animals are more equal than others."

Napoleon, the dictator pig in George Orwell's Animal Farm

The George Orwell classic, "Animal Farm," features an imaginary farm in which the animals rebel against their human masters, demanding equality, with the catchy slogan, "Four legs good, two legs bad." Once they have achieved their revolutionary goals, the pigs brutally repress the other animals, claiming that some animals are "more equal" than others.

Orwell's powerful, but not so idyllic animal fable was based on the Bolshevik revolution and the rise of Communism, but there are analogies that can be made concerning the conflict between Israel and its enemies, as well, especially as it relates to American foreign policy.

US State Department spokeswoman Jen Psaki has implicitly declared that American foreign policy has entered the surreal realm of Animal Farm, with her criticism yesterday of Israel after the IDF (Israel Defense Forces) shot dead a 17-year-old Arab teenager who was throwing firebombs at Israeli motorists near the community of Ofra, here in the region of Samaria (the northern part of the so-called West Bank). The young attacker, apparently caught in the middle of the attack, happens to be an American citizen, thereby raising American ire above the usual levels. Said Psaki, "The United States expresses its deepest condolences to the family of a US citizen minor, who was killed by the Israeli Defense Forces during clashes in Silwad (an Arab village near Ofra) on October 24." Calling for "a speedy and transparent investigation," Psaki said officials from the US consulate in Jerusalem were in touch with the family of the slain youth.

While it's certainly understandable for the American government to show some concern for all American citizens, even those who may have committed crimes, such public concern in this context seems obscene when viewed in context. The young attacker wasn't killed "in clashes" – he was throwing petrol bombs at Israelis, seeking to maim or kill them. Furthermore, the juxtaposition of events is even more disturbing, coming on the heels of the Islamic terrorist attack in Jerusalem just a day earlier, when a three-month-old Jewish baby Chaya Zissel Braun was murdered by a rampaging terrorist who slammed a car directly into a crowd of pedestrians coming off a Jerusalem light rail train, killing the infant and wounding eight others.

Baby Chaya was an American citizen. While there was an eventual statement from the US State Department after the attack, the fact that the murdered infant was an American citizen was only mentioned as an afterthought. Which brings us back to the surreal world of Animal Farm –

Are American citizens who carry out terrorist attacks "more equal" than American citizen victims of terrorist attacks?

Is the teenage firebomber who throws petrol bombs at Israeli vehicles seeking to kill babies deserving of more concern than the baby victims themselves?

Where are the US State Department's expressions of deep concern for the families of the victims?

There seems to be a warped sense of values here that is badly in need of correction.

What Will The Goyim Say?

"The Lord is with me; I shall not be afraid. What can mere mortals do to me?"

Psalms 118:6

The announcement yesterday on Israel's Channel Two, of a tentative deal between Prime Minister Binyamin Netanyahu and Economy Minister Naftali Bennett to end the unofficial freeze on the building of homes in Judea and Samaria (the so-called West Bank) and eastern Jerusalem, has stirred up political emotions to a fever pitch, both at home and abroad.

This new commotion comes on the heels of the disturbing winds blowing from the east, as King Abdullah of Jordan equated Islamic extremism with "Zionist extremism" in remarks regarding the fight against terrorism. This statement by the king, who was clearly looking over his Islamic shoulder at the growing number of Jihadists in his kingdom and beyond, was especially striking, due to the absence of the word "Israel," the country with which he supposedly has a peace treaty.

Abdullah's equating of ISIS beheadings with the building of homes for growing families in Israel's capital city was troubling enough, but was quickly followed by the outrageous threat delivered by Jordan's ambassador to Israel, Walid Obeidat, who declared, referring to Israel's granting of building permits to Jews, "All such acts are incompatible with international law and international humanitarian law and if allowed to continue will ultimately imperil the treaty."

These words were spoken in Tel Aviv at an anniversary event commemorating the peace treaty between Israel and Jordan.

Much closer to home, two senior Cabinet members warned Netanyahu that more construction in Jewish settlements would further inflame already tense ties with the United States. Justice Minister Tzipi Livni blasted the Netanyahu-Bennett deal, saying that it was "irresponsible from both a diplomatic and security standpoint," while Finance Minister Yair Lapid added that while he is in principal not opposed to construction inside the settlement blocs, more construction "at this stage would lead to a serious crisis in ties with the United States, and it would harm Israel's international standing." As could be expected, the hard-core Israeli left-wing opposition came out with their usual anti-Zionist, almost anti-Semitic statements, expressing anger at any increase in Jewish housing:

> *"Netanyahu is selling the State of Israel's diplomatic interests in exchange for a few more months in the prime minister's chair," read a statement issued by the Labor Party. "If this is Netanyahu's idea of a solution to the diplomatic crisis and to the high cost of housing, then he has completely lost direction."*

Contrary to the Labor Party pundits' official statement, opening up the housing markets to building in Israel's heartland communities would, indeed, help to end the shortage of housing in the country as a whole, and it would bring down prices, but then again, labor socialists don't believe in free markets, do they?

Putting all of these vociferous declarations together, we see some common themes that are actually quite instructive, for the opposite reasons than those for which they were intended. The excessive concern for what the goyim (Gentiles or non-Jews) will say has long been a source of tension in Zionism, almost across the political spectrum. Yes, we do live in this world and it is critical that we cooperate with Gentiles, and specifically with countries or individuals that are friendly to us and want to support and further Israel's national rebirth in the Land of Israel. However, that doesn't mean that we have to give in to the dictates of those who act against the fundamentals of Zionism, which by definition refers to the rebuilding of the Land of Israel as the national home of the Jewish people. Caving in to those dictates by halting building in Israel's capital, Jerusalem, and in Israel's biblical heartland, Judea and Samaria, is anti-Zionist, hence anti-Israel and a blow to Israel's sovereignty.

Let King Abdullah of Jordan and his homeboys continue to babble on about how they will cancel the peace treaty. They need it far more than we do. Instead of criticizing us, they should be forever thanking us for letting their Hashemite family, which was imported from the Arabian Peninsula by the British and placed on the throne, to remain in power on what is actually the eastern side of the Land of Israel.

After 66 years as a reestablished sovereign nation, it's time that we act in our interests, first and foremost, and learn to have thick skin when verbally attacked. Our opponents will scream and yell and even condemn, but they won't do much more than that. Let the rebuilding continue, onward and upward!

Nuclear Deal Or Not:
The View From Iran

"Israel is a wound on the body of the world of Islam that must be destroyed."

Hassan Rouhani, President of Iran

A s events heat up in Jerusalem with the recent upsurge in terrorist attacks, as well as the ongoing political missiles being aimed at Prime Minister Netanyahu by the Obama administration, there is another, more ominous threat simmering below the surface that could potentially set the Middle East on fire. As we approach the November 24th deadline for a deal that is intended to halt or slow down Iran's nuclear race, the recurring question is back in the news – Will the United States and the other nations participating in the negotiations with Iran, sign an agreement that will allow the Islamic regime to go forward in developing nuclear weapons capability?

Despite Israel's persistent warnings to the negotiating nations that a bad deal is far worse than no deal, the Iranian regime seems more confident than ever that it will be able to get a deal that will enable it to move forward with its goal of becoming a nuclear power.

In a very revealing interview with Iran's Fars News Agency, as reported by MEMRI (the Middle East Media Research Institute), Iranian President Hassan Rouhani's advisor, Ali Younesi, declared that "the Obama administration desperately needs a substantial achievement to show for its term in office, and therefore this is the time to pressure it ... I am not so optimistic about the nuclear negotiations, but both sides do want it to yield results. The Americans want this more than other countries." This American eagerness for a deal has been evident all along, as all requests from Israel to strengthen sanctions and to leave a realistic military option on the table have been rejected by the Obama administration.

Finally, in Younesi's most revealing statement, which exposes Iran's strategy for all to see, he declares, "Obama is the weakest president the US has ever had, because he has suffered humiliating defeat in this region, and his term in office saw the coming of the Islamic awakening that dealt the Americans the greatest defeat. It is during Obama's term in office that terrorism spread to the greatest extent. During these eight years, America suffered immense defeat, and that is why he wants to reach an agreement." Furthermore, Iran's parliament speaker, Ali Larijani, said on Sunday that Iran would not accept any limits on its nuclear program except those "within the logical framework of transparency (measures) in the nuclear technology," Iran's Tasnim News Agency reported.

Can it be any clearer? Iran is going full speed ahead for the nuclear bomb and believes that Obama's weakness will enable it to achieve its goals through these negotiations. Barring a preemptive surprise attack, expect an agreement to be reached that will place some limitations on Iran's nuclear program, but that will allow it to move forward towards nuclear weapons capability.

Needless to say, such a deal will greatly heighten the chances of a major military confrontation between Israel and Iran. Given Obama's proven hostility towards Israel, such a scenario doesn't seem to concern him too much.

Ever Heard Of Alarm Clocks?

"Every human being is entitled to courtesy and consideration."

Margaret Chase Smith, American politician

The faction chairman of the Yisrael Beytenu party, Robert Ilatov, has submitted a bill in the Knesset calling for a ban on the usage of public loudspeaker systems to call Muslims to prayer – called the Adhan in Arabic – and any other sound emanating from a religious institution that is considered noise pollution.

The five times daily Muslim call to pray from the mosques, often as early as 4:00 a.m., has long been a terrible disturbance for Israelis who live near Arab towns or neighborhoods. The loudspeaker system used for these announcements can be heard clearly in the early morning hours when most people are trying to sleep, and therefore, it is a rude disruption of sleep and a blatant infringement on the rights of hundreds of thousands of Israelis.

MK Ilatov explained that many countries in the world have placed constraints on noise pollution and noise levels, including several European countries that have specifically restricted the use of these loudspeakers as an infringement on the rights of individuals. In Amsterdam and in Austria, it can only be broadcast on Fridays, and at a reduced decibel level. In France, public loudspeakers may not be used at all, while in Belgium the muezzin's call cannot be broadcast. As for Switzerland, mosques are no longer allowed to build minarets, the tower from which the call to prayer emanates.

The Muslims are crying foul, complaining that their

religious freedom is being impinged upon. Perhaps someone should point out to them that many Jews also get up for daily prayers, often as early as 5:00 in the morning at certain times of the year. No Jew would ever request a public wake-up call that would undoubtedly disturb those other people who for some strange reason would like to wake up a bit later. We Jews have actually found a novel way of waking up – It's called an alarm clock.

Nonetheless, the issue is much greater than an unwanted morning wake-up call. Israelis, Americans, and other folks who believe in freedom should understand that this "call to prayer" controversy is symptomatic of a much larger problem that is coming soon to a country near you. As the Muslim populations grow, the demand for Sharia law (the oppressive Muslim law that demands submission to Islam) will grow. When that happens, wife-beating, death sentences to those who leave Islam, and a ban on all non-Muslim forms of worship will become the norm in every Islamic-dominated country.

We don't need a 4:00 a.m. wake-up call to see the writing on the wall. The Islamic race to Sharia law is speeding up, especially in the Western countries. We Israelis should set a good example by respecting the rights and needs of Israel's citizens. Yes to alarm clocks, and yes to this excellent bill that should quickly be approved into law.

Declare Abbas An Enemy Of Israel

"Are you tired of sand being kicked in your face? I promise you new muscles in days!"

Charles Atlas, body-building entrepreneur

Mahmoud Abbas has been spitting in Israel's face for years and we've been acting like it's raining. Will Israel's political leadership finally name him for the enemy that he is?

In his latest outrage, a condolence letter to the Israeli-Arab family of the would-be murderer of Temple Mount activist Yehuda Glick, Abbas brazenly condemned Israel for killing the terrorist:

> *"We received with anger the announcement about the despicable crime perpetrated by the gangs of killing and terror in the Israeli occupation army, against the son, Muataz Ibrahim Hijazi, who rose to the heavens as a martyr for the defense of the rights of the Palestinian nation and the holy places."*

In response, Prime Minister Netanyahu "condemned" Abbas's letter and demanded that the European countries do the same. With all due respect to Mr. Netanyahu, this former "partner for peace" is a vile hater of Israel, always has been, and he leads a people who are an enemy of Israel at least on the level of the Philistines of biblical times. It's not an accident that they have been represented through the years by Hamas, Fatah, and Islamic Jihad. That is what they want. Sure, they will gladly take Bibi's monetary handouts and accept his efforts to improve their standard of living so they can become hi-tech entrepreneurs in Ramallah, but they will still call for, and work towards, Israel's destruction.

There is no longer any excuse for pathetic condemnations from Netanyahu and his colleagues that do nothing except to embolden the enemy. We have been complaining to the world about PA incitement already for twenty years. Enough is enough.

The time has come for action:

1. Declare the Palestinian Authority an enemy of Israel.

2. Declare the Oslo Accords that established the PA to be null and void. Publicly announce the PA violations that led to this decision.

3. Stand firm against all of the shrieks and condemnations that will follow. No breast-beating or excuses are necessary for a morally correct action.

4. Immediately end all cooperation and contact with the PA and all money transfers to the PA.

5. Immediately adopt the conclusions of the Levy Report, which gives clear, solid legal backing to the Israeli presence in Judea and Samaria, as the new basis for government policy in the biblical heartland of Israel.

The reestablishment of Israel as a sovereign nation in its land necessitates adherence to the principles of self-preservation and the primacy of Israel's interests, not as perceived by, nor as defined by the Western nations that are, with a couple of notable exceptions, fair weather friends who don't stand with us politically when the going gets tough.

Abbas is an enemy of Israel. Let's call him that and draw the proper conclusions from that declaration.

Shameful Lack Of National Pride

"There cannot be discrimination – not against Jews and not against Arabs."

Binyamin Netanyahu, Prime Minister of Israel

In June of 1967, at the climax of the Six Day War, Israel's paratroops commander Motta Gur, somewhat out of character, emotionally announced the words that still resonate to this day, "The Temple Mount is in our hands." Shortly thereafter, Defense Minister Moshe Dayan, fearing the potential Islamic and international outcry, shamefully robbed Israel of at least part of its great victory, by handing over the keys of the holiest place in Judaism to the Muslim Wakf of Jordan.

For those who are unaware, this holy site is the plateau on which the two Temples of Israel had stood for hundreds of years. Below it, at its western retaining wall, Jews had shed bitter tears for centuries. For that reason, it was known to many as the Wailing Wall. Since that miraculous week in 1967, when all of eastern Jerusalem fell back into Israel's hands, it is known to all as the Western Wall. Now that Jerusalem had been liberated, there was no more need to cry.

Despite the fact that the Western Wall has become somewhat of a shrine for the Jewish people and all visitors from around the world, the Temple Mount above it has remained the ultimate symbol of Israel's former unified sovereign kingdom, with its capital in Jerusalem.

In recent weeks, we have witnessed massive rioting and violent vandalism by Muslims in Jerusalem, coupled with a spate of terror attacks, including the killing of a young baby and others, as well as the very symbolic murder attempt on Yehuda Glick, whose only "crime" was his public activism on behalf of the right of Jews to pray on the Temple Mount. Israel's political leadership quickly responded to that blatant act of targeted terrorism by temporarily closing the Temple Mount to all, an act of pathetic political weakness that encouraged the Arab nations, including the British-appointed illegal country on the other side of the Jordan River, to cry foul, complaining that no Muslim prayer rights should be restricted. This disingenuous complaint is heard loud and clear from the Islamic freedom of worship hypocrites, even though Jews have not been allowed to pray on the Mount since its liberation forty-seven years ago.

Given this background, it is actually quite shocking that Prime Minister Binyamin Netanyahu has responded to the subsequent Jordanian threats by promising King Abdullah that Israel will protect the status quo on the Mount. Such a feckless arrangement panders to the Muslim threats and encourages more violence, riots, and terrorism on Israel's citizens. Sadly, and despite his tough image outside of Israel, Netanyahu has been known to often cringe under pressure, quickly caving in when the nations of the world launch their unfair attacks on Israel's sovereignty.

One can only hope, and yes pray, that we will soon see a reversal of this terribly discriminatory policy under which a Jew cannot visibly speak to his Creator on the Temple Mount without being arrested. As one who spent many of his younger years in the United States, presumably experiencing its widespread freedom of worship, Netanyahu should know better than to continue such a shameful policy.

A political leader is expected to make decisions based on the national interest, always keeping human rights and freedoms in mind. The status quo on the Temple Mount is a crude violation of both and should be immediately changed.

Chief Rabbis And Spiritual Leadership

"Let the wise hear and increase in learning, and the one who understands obtain guidance."

Proverbs 1:5

Chief Rabbi Yitzhak Yosef, speaking at the funeral of a boy killed in one of the recent terrorist attacks in Jerusalem, actually blamed the rise in Islamic terrorism on Jews who act to assert freedom of worship.

He blasted Jews who go up to the Temple Mount, declaring that they are responsible for the recent surge in terrorist attacks. "We must stop this," he said, directing his comments at those Jewish worshipers who have the "chutzpah" to ascend to the holiest site in Judaism, and called on them to refrain from doing so, stating ominously, "Only then will the bloodshed end."

One could be forgiven for mistakenly thinking that Mahmoud Abbas or Khaled Mashal had made such an outrageous statement, which sounds almost like an implied threat to launch more terrorist attacks. For all of his Torah knowledge, doesn't the holy rabbi understand that such statements, in effect blaming the victims, will encourage further terrorist attacks by actually justifying the Muslims' excuse for such attacks?

Furthermore, doesn't he realize that Israel has been reestablished as a sovereign nation in the Land of Israel, and that we, as a responsible sovereign nation, should respect the principle of religious freedom for all? Should the Islamic attempts to riot, to wound, and to kill Jews be that which deters us from asserting that freedom?

As if that wasn't enough, the Haredi (ultra-Orthodox) Rabbi Yosef continued his diatribe, and in an obvious dig at religious Zionist rabbis, many of whom support some form of Jewish prayer rights on the site, proclaimed that "fourth-rate rabbis cannot dispute (the rulings of) the sages of Israel." One has to wonder which "fourth-rate rabbis" he was referring to.

Rabbi Yosef may believe that it is wrong for Jews to ascend to the Mount at this time, and it is certainly his right to believe that, but there are many esteemed rabbis in Israel who disagree. Long is the list of great rabbis, including former Chief Rabbis Shlomo Goren and Mordechai Eliyahu, of blessed memory, who have supported, and continue to support such visits. Crudely resorting to name-calling towards some of the great rabbis of our generation, rather than simply expressing his differing opinion while showing respect towards those rabbis, is at best, poor judgment on his part. He is, after all, the chief rabbi of all of Israel and should be a unifying spiritual leader who, at the very least, respects that there are those rabbis who disagree. Hopefully, he will think carefully before spewing out such inaccurate and biased nonsense in the future.

The Kahane Legacy

"I'm a catalyst for change. You can't be an outsider and be successful over 30 years without leaving a certain amount of scar tissue around the place."

Rupert Murdoch, publisher

There has long been a debate over the legacy of former Prime Minister Yitzhak Rabin. The anniversary of his assassination having recently passed, the issue periodically reemerges about whether we should memorialize and reflexively praise the "Oslo Prime Minister", or whether we should sharply criticize the many questionable aspects of his legacy. I, for one, prefer to focus on the importance of unity, as it relates to the horrible assassination of a prime minister, most likely by another Jew, and to use that focus to increase respect and cooperation, despite the many differences within the Israeli populace.

Another legacy often overlooked in the general Israeli public is that of former MK Rabbi Meir Kahane, whose memorial day was observed this week. Kahane's legacy has become especially relevant in these past few years, as we have faced an increase in the frequency of wars; as well as in the past few weeks, during which we have experienced a sharp rise in terror attacks. Kahane's legacy, despite the red light that it sets off in many mainstream Israelis, should be carefully examined, in order to learn important lessons that may help us to confront some of today's existential challenges.

Rabbi Kahane was steeped in Torah knowledge, which

he acquired from both ultra-Orthodox (Haredi) and Zionist rabbis, as well as from the great sages of the generations, but he also possessed extensive secular knowledge and held two higher degrees from American universities. A strong defender of Jews in America, in the former Soviet Union, and elsewhere, Kahane founded the Jewish Defense League and coined the slogan, "Never Again", which meant that never again should Jews remain passive when Jewish lives are at stake. He was an extremely passionate Zionist who proudly recited the Hallel prayer on Israel's yearly Independence Day (with a blessing) and he eventually made Aliyah to Israel.

In Israel, as before, Kahane had his many detractors and he had an aggressive political style that delighted many of his followers. However, that same characteristic also turned away many would-be supporters. Nonetheless, he was an undeniably effective catalyst, whose message resonates to this day. Kahane dared to sound the warning thirty years ago about a then rapidly growing birthrate in a hostile Arab population, coupled with a then dormant Jewish birthrate. Thankfully, this is one warning that hasn't fully come to fruition, as Jewish Israelis are now returning to traditional family life in increasing numbers and the birthrate gap is quickly closing, an impressive trend that is evident across the religious spectrum. Whether this change was influenced by the warnings of Rabbi Kahane, and/or those of other vocal transfer advocates like the late MK Rechavam Ze'vi, who was assassinated by Palestinian terrorists, the message of the demographic danger was apparently well absorbed by the Israeli public.

Alongside Kahane's insistence on a policy of transfer/ expulsion for the enemies of Israel and his strong advocacy of a no-tolerance policy towards terrorism, he was also passionate in his encouragement of Jews to return to their religious roots, and was second to none in his urging of assimilated Jews living in the Diaspora to return home to Israel, and especially to its idealistic young communities in the biblical heartland of Judea and Samaria.

He was often called a racist, as well as far worse names that cannot be mentioned here, by a left-controlled media that despised him, and refused to engage in honest debate on the real issues that he was raising, and he also wasn't trusted by some right-leaning Israelis, some of whom considered the often abrasive Kahane style in confronting Israel's Arab population to be counter-productive. Legitimate arguments could have certainly been made about the effectiveness or correctness of Rabbi Kahane's tactics, but the questions that he raised about the innate disloyalty of the Israeli-Arab (now mostly Muslim) population were relevant and critical even then and needed to be discussed, not ignored. Instead, the other Israeli politicians, in an obscene disregard for freedom of speech, voted to silence him and banned him from the Knesset. Several years later, he was murdered in New York by El-Sayid Nosair, a Muslim terrorist with ties to the first World Trade Center bombing and to al-Qaeda terrorists.

We see today that many of Rabbi Kahane's positive ideas have been internalized and adopted by current Knesset members and by other influential people in Israeli society. Not all are willing to acknowledge that influence for fear of being slandered themselves as "Kahanists" or "extremists" by a still left-dominated media, but that really doesn't matter, because any message is always more important than the messenger. And that is the value of a catalyst, as well as the significance of his legacy.

The Suicidal Swedes And
The Recognition of "Palestine"

"Remember, democracy never lasts long. It soon wastes, exhausts, and murders itself. There never was a democracy yet that did not commit suicide."

John Adams, American President

Many Israelis were angered and disturbed by Sweden's recent perplexing, yet bold move, declaring its recognition of a State of Palestine that never existed, doesn't exist, and doesn't deserve to exist. Why would Sweden choose to be the first country to go on record as politically supporting what would undeniably become another Islamic terrorist state? Why would a country known for its liberated women, choose to become the first European country to encourage the rise of what would certainly be another repressive Islamic country with laws allowing men to beat their wives, to have multiple wives, and to rape underage girls?

Israel will survive this political travesty, but Sweden is in trouble. After a recent speaking tour in the formerly "blond" country, I am more convinced than ever that something must be done quickly, if Sweden, a country whose indigenous population has almost stopped having children, is to prevent being overrun by its rapidly growing Muslim population. The situation is no better in many other countries in Western Europe, where 20-25% Muslim populations are becoming more common in many cities, where street crime is rampant, and where police don't dare to tread. The impending Islamic takeover of nuclear Europe does not bode well for the cause of freedom in the rest of the world either, not for women, not for men and children, nor for anyone who believes in freedom and tolerance.

So how is this connected to the Swedish recognition of Israel? The decision to recognize "Palestine" was no doubt influenced by the sharp increase in the amount of Muslim voters in that Scandinavian nation and the leftist Social Democrats' perceived need to pander to that population.

However, the problem is much deeper and is clearly evident throughout Europe and the United States, in fact throughout all of Western civilization. There is a strange sort of unofficial collusion between secular leftists and Islamic ideologues. This seemingly inexplicable partnership can be seen in the universities, in the media, in politics, and on the streets. The Left wants a modified secular communism/socialism or a free-wheeling hedonism in which anything goes and truth is in the eye of the beholder. Islam, on the other hand, wants only to change Western civilization into an Islamic civilization.

And that is the key binding element. Both the secular Left and the Islamic ideologues want to bring down Judeo-Christian civilization in the short term. They will worry about their sharp differences later on. Israel, being the cradle of Western civilization with its proud and growing Jewish identity and its manifest prophecy in action, is perceived as an obstacle in the way of the goal of those two extreme self-destructive forces that are rising in the West.

The problem for the near-sighted secular leftists in Sweden and elsewhere is that once the sons of Ishmael have attained power, they will rape, slaughter, and behead their non-Muslim countrymen and women, just as they have done in the Middle East to the Jews and to anyone else who gets in their way. Sadly, the Jewish value of mercy is unheard of in the religion of "Jihad".

A Europe that wants to survive the Islamic demographic nightmare that awaits it, needs a more sensible strategy than pathetically pandering for votes on the road to national suicide. Sweden and the rest of Western civilization would be very wise to reconnect with the biblical roots of Western civilization, The best way to do that is by firmly bonding with the biblical nation – with Israel and the Jewish people – standing with us as we confront our enemies, and showing respect for Israel's heritage.

The road to Western survival runs through Israel.

Five Steps To End
The Latest Wave Of Terror

"Insanity: doing the same thing over and over again and expecting different results."

Albert Einstein, Nobel Laureate

T he brutal terrorist attack in a synagogue in the Har Nof neighborhood of Jerusalem has left five Israelis dead and many others wounded. We have clearly returned to the days of 2000-2004, when terrorist attacks on Israeli civilians were an almost daily occurrence and the tension in the air could be sliced with a knife. As a resident of Samaria and a terror victim myself, I will never forget those days, when mothers and fathers often didn't know if their children were coming home and children were traumatized for life by the sudden loss of parents and siblings, viciously gunned down and bombed to death by employees of the Palestinian Authority.

From those bitter days, ten years have passed and we are back to square one. I have always predicted that the terrorist attacks would be renewed when Mahmoud Abbas was ready to turn on the faucet. That day has arrived and once again, the same tired techniques are being used to defeat the latest terror war that was never really defeated. Our political leadership is once again destroying the homes of the individual terrorists, using Israeli intelligence to track down the shooters and bombers, and is giving the okay for more Israeli citizens to carry guns.

However, while these tactics can be useful, they will not end this latest terror war because we are not recognizing it as a war. Terrorism is not an enemy – it is a strategy. The Palestinian Authority is the enemy that has been financing and encouraging this latest terror war with its money and statements, and it should be treated like the enemy that it is.

The following steps should be taken at this stage:

1. Enter Ramallah and take control of Abbas's Mukata headquarters.

2. Seize all of the latest documents (we already have the old ones) proving that Abbas has been financing and encouraging terrorism.

3. Level the Mukata to the ground.

4. Declare the Oslo Accords, hence the Palestinian Authority as well, null and void.

5. Begin the painstaking process of collecting all weapons from all of the terrorist organizations that are active in Judea, Samaria, and Jerusalem.

Fighting a war against a terrorist enemy is not easy, nor is it pleasant. Terrorism is a ruthless strategy that can only be defeated by similar ruthlessness. Admittedly, the Jewish people are not known for such ruthlessness, which is quite out of character, but there are times when it is necessary and unfortunately, that is the only language that the Palestinian Authority and its residents will understand.

Go forth O' Israel and fear not the wrath of the Arab nation, which will scatter like the wind when they see that we are on the offensive.

Afterword

As *Sparks From Zion* goes to press, the current governing coalition here in Israel has fallen and new elections are scheduled to be held in March of 2015. Already the political jockeying has begun, with the secular Left reportedly forming a merger of parties. Their goal – to prevent the right-wing and the religious parties from gaining an expected majority that will be loyal to the Land of Israel and its heritage.

Obviously, there will be a lot to write about in the weeks and months ahead...

About The Author

David Rubin is a former mayor of Shiloh, Israel – in the region of Samaria, which together with Judea, is known to much of the world as the West Bank. He is the founder and president of Shiloh Israel Children's Fund (SICF) – dedicated to healing the trauma of children who have been victims of terrorist attacks, as well as rebuilding the biblical heartland of Israel through the children.

SICF was established after Rubin and his three-year-old son were wounded in a vicious terrorist attack while driving home from Jerusalem. Rubin vowed to retaliate – not with hatred, nor with anger, but with compassion – in order to affect positive change for Israel and its children.

Rubin's first book is "God, Israel, & Shiloh: Returning to the Land", which tells the story of the very human struggles and triumphs of Israel's complex history, dating back to slavery in Egypt and continuing up to the present. Rubin describes Israel's miraculous return to its biblical heartland, and the subsequent challenge of its residents to rebuild, despite the constant threat of terrorism and the trauma of the many terrorist attacks that have affected their communities.

Rubin's second book is the groundbreaking "The Islamic Tsunami: Israel and America in the Age of Obama", which boldly exposes the danger to Israel, America and Judeo-Christian civilization posed by the Islamic ideologues and their odd collusion with the far secular Left.

His most recent book is "Peace For Peace: Israel in the New Middle East", which scans the history of the peace process and explains why it hasn't worked and how it can work – by taking into account biblical principles, historical precedent, and common sense. All of these books are as relevant today as when they were first published.

David Rubin is a regular and very popular blogger on Arutz Sheva, otherwise known as www.IsraelNationalNews.com and his articles have appeared in numerous other publications. A featured speaker throughout North America, Europe, and Israel, David Rubin is a frequent guest commentator on national and international radio and television programs.

Born and raised in Brooklyn, New York, Rubin resides in Israel with his wife and children on a hilltop overlooking the site of Ancient Shiloh. This is the hallowed ground where the Tabernacle of Israel stood for 369 years in the time of Joshua, Hannah, and Samuel the Prophet.

Other Books By David Rubin

Available online at www.DavidRubinIsrael.com/books/
~ Phone orders 1-800-431-1579 ~ Or at a bookstore near you!

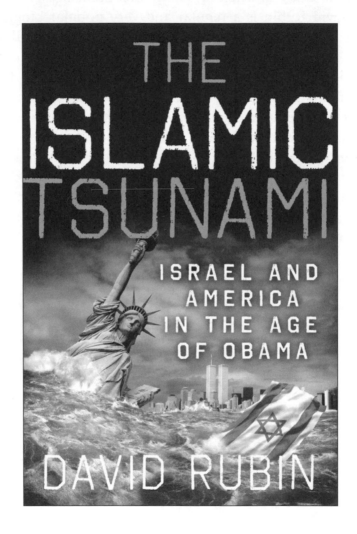

The Islamic Tsunami
Israel And America In The Age Of Obama
ISBN: 978-0-9829067-0-5